The Crafty Diva's D.I.Y. Stylebook

A Grrrl's Guide to Cool Creations You Can Make, Show Off, and Share

by
Kathy Cano Murillo

Illustrated by
Carrie Wheeler

Photography by
John Samora

Watson-Guptill Publications/New York

This book is dedicated to my
favorite crafty diva of all time:
my daughter, Maya Murillo.

Senior Editor: Julie Mazur
Design: pink design, inc.
Production Manager: Ellen Greene
Text set in 10-point Bernhard Gothic Book

First published in 2004 by
Watson-Guptill Publications,
a division of VNU Business Media, Inc.
770 Broadway, New York, NY 10003
www.watsonguptill.com

Library of Congress Cataloging-in-Publication Data

Cano-Murillo, Kathy.
    The crafty diva's D.I.Y. stylebook : a grrrl's [sic] guide to cool creations you can make, show off, and share /
Kathy Cano Murillo ; illustrated by Carrie Wheeler ; photography by John Samora.
        p. cm.
    Includes index.
    Summary: Provides step-by-step instructions for a variety of crafts, coded as easy, moderate, or difficult, and organized
by such styles as "animal lover," "beautiful bohemian," "party priestess," and "flashy fashionista."
    ISBN 0-8230-6993-1
1. Handicraft for girls—Juvenile literature. [1. Handicraft.] I. Title: Crafty diva's do-it-yourself stylebook. II. Wheeler, Carrie,
ill. III. Title.
    TT171.C35 2004
    745.5—dc22
                        2003020206

Printed in Malaysia

First printing, 2004

1 2 3 4 5 6 7 8 / 11 10 09 08 07 06 05 04

Every effort has been made to ensure that the material presented in this book is accurate. Readers are strongly advised
to read product labels, follow manufacturers' instructions, and seek prompt medical attention for any injury. The publisher
disclaims liability for injuries, losses, untoward results, or any other damages that may result from the use of information
in this book.

Meet the Original Crafty Divas

Author **Kathy Cano Murillo**'s passion for arts and crafts began in grade school, when she thought she made the best chalk painting in the class but the teacher didn't think it was good enough to hang in the cafeteria on parents' night. Totally crushed, Kathy vowed that from that day forward she would make her mark on the crafty world with glitter sprinkles and high-gloss varnish. She is now an entertainment reporter and crafts columnist for *The Arizona Republic* newspaper. She has written two other craft books, *Making Shadow Boxes and Shrines* and *La Casa Loca: Latino Style Comes Home*. She also designs a line of Chicano pop art. Visit her Web site at www.CraftyChica.com or e-mail her at kathymurillo@hotmail.com. Kathy lives in Phoenix, Arizona.

Illustrator **Carrie Wheeler** is a sassy Web designer and online fashion editor. Although she has been drawing her entire life, this is her first book. Visit her Web site at www.CrackingGood.com. Carrie lives in Phoenix, Arizona.

Photographer **John Samora** has been shooting pictures of everything from rock stars to fashion models for more than twenty years, for clients including Fender Guitars, *National Geographic,* and *Time* magazine. When he doesn't have a camera to his eye, John plays the harmonica and sings in the Phoenix-based blues band Big Nick and the Gila Monsters. Visit his Web site at www.JohnSamora.com. John lives in Phoenix, Arizona.

CONTENTS

INTRODUCTION:
Are You a Crafty Diva?

The answer is "yes" if you...

* Think sprinkling glitter on everything makes it better.
* Truly believe arts and crafts are the paths to world peace.
* Never leave home without a six-pack of fruit-scented markers.
* Dream of becoming a clothing designer, artist, decorator, or stylist.

If you can relate to any of the above, *chica,* you are true crafting royalty—with a dash of attitude, of course. Welcome to your ultimate crafty adventure! This sparkling page-turner is a confetti-filled piñata party of do-it-yourself projects dedicated to you, the crafty diva. Why? Because, sister, your style is cooler than a pineapple snow cone. Your personality is cuter than a pocket Neopet. Your flava for accessories is tastier than spicy pepperoni pizza with a side of ranch dressing. And your mood? It changes channels quicker than your remote control. Those are reasons enough for you to indulge in some artful "me-time."

The true meaning of "crafty"

The first lesson in this classroom of creativity is to embrace the word "crafty." Learn it. Know it. Live it. Is your first thought glitter glue and animal-print trim? Good job, you're on the right track. However, being crafty is also a state of mind. It means amping up your imagination to look beyond the basic uses of everyday objects. Where others see a boring lamp, you see a glittery light fixture. While others toss out their empty mint tins, you save them and make super-secret picture frames. Crafty divas *always* think twice before throwing something away.

But hold on, why make something if you can just buy it? True, we all love to spend time at the mall drooling over the latest goods. But unless you're Britney Spears, there's no way you can buy it all. Fact is, lots of the cute things you see in stores can be almost duplicated in your own crafty quarters—with a thrifty twist, of course! By exercising your noggin with tips from this book, you'll discover that there are gobs of cheap, easy ways to bring your one-of-a-kind ideas to life. Besides, self-expression is priceless, wouldn't you say?

At your fingertips

Warmed up yet for the sensational stuff ahead? Before you reach for the art smock, take this revealing quiz to pinpoint your individual style. You'll also want to check out Doodling 101 (page 136) to learn about drawing funny flowers, faces, and letters. And to make sure you do things right (you know, like how to use needle-nose pliers without pinching your nose?), be sure to read the Crafty Essentials section starting on page 8. It comes with a handy built-in ruler, everything you ever wanted to know about glue, a list of dos and don'ts, and so much more!

QUIZ: What's Your Style?

We've organized the crafty creations in this book by "style," so here's a little quiz to point you in the right direction. Odds are, most of you will see a bit of yourself in each personality type. Us girls are fickle. One day we need to be alone to think about the meaning of life, and the next minute we're standing on our bed playing air guitar. So no worries, okay? Here we go:

1. If you could do anything you wanted to for your birthday, you would choose:

  a. A quiet night at home with the family.

  b. A slumber party with your best friends and a karaoke machine.

  c. A weekend trip to Beverly Hills for a shopping spree and celebrity sightings.

2. Your school locker is covered with:

  a. Pictures from when you volunteered with your family at the local pet adopt-a-thon.

  b. Photos of you in the front row at the latest pop concert.

  c. Ripped-out pages from magazines showing clothes you like.

3. You think TV is:

  a. Not as much fun as reading a good book.

  b. The best invention since chocolate-flavored lip balm.

  c. Great for catching up on all the latest Hollywood gossip.

4. When it comes to gym class at school, you:

  a. Ask the coach to please make sure your soccer game won't hurt any nearby plants or animals.

  b. Arrive ready for action, complete with moisturizing sunscreen and proper uniform, hoping to get chosen as team captain.

  c. Look at it as a good way to chat about the latest singer to get booted from *American Idol*.

5. After a day at the mall, you come home with:

  a. A bag of goodies that you plan to give as gifts.

  b. A vintage Madonna T-shirt, handmade soap, and a new swimsuit.

  c. Fashion magazines, a new cell-phone case, and rhinestone bracelets.

Scoring: Give yourself 1 point for each "a" answer, 2 points for each "b" answer, and 3 points for each "c" answer. Read below to see which chapters match your vibe.

5–7 points: You are a sweetheart! Your family is true to your heart, you like quiet time, and you respect animals and Mother Nature. Check out these chapters: Animal Lover, Artful Bookworm, Beautiful Bohemian, Family Bonder, Garden Goddess, Happy Homebody, and Neat Freak.

8–12 points: You are one busy gal. That happenin' world of yours revolves around excellent friends, sports, and drum lessons. You will dig: Beauty Chemist, Surf Girl, Faithful Friend, Party Priestess, Sporty Sista, and Rowdy Rock Star.

13–15 points: "Diva" is your middle name! Heads turn when you walk into a room because you're wearing the most stylin' threads. Do you own anything that doesn't shine? Nope. Lookie here: Drama Queen, Flashy Fashionista, Hollywood Diva, Spa Guru, Social Butterfly, Teenybopper, and Jewelry Hound.

CRAFTY ESSENTIALS:
A Must-Read

It's true that there are no rules to art. But like writing a short story for English class, there *are* guidelines. You are now ordered by the craft police to read and follow the tips below. In fact, read them twice. Not only will they help you be a better artist, they'll also keep you safe and help you save money on your supplies. I've also recommended certain brands because after many years of crafting, I've found them to be the best and the most affordable.

It's a good idea to make a trip to the craft store ahead of time to stock up on supplies—there's nothing worse than wanting to make something and not having the materials!

Tip Save some change by asking Mom to keep an eye out for craft-store newspaper ads and special sales.

Paints and Pens

You can't call yourself a crafty diva without dabbling in the colored stuff. Paints and pens are your one-way ticket to makeover heaven, whether it's on fabric, wood, or paper. So let's get educated.

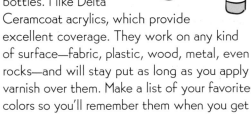

Craft acrylic paint: These water-based, nontoxic paints come in 2-ounce bottles. I like Delta Ceramcoat acrylics, which provide excellent coverage. They work on any kind of surface—fabric, plastic, wood, metal, even rocks—and will stay put as long as you apply varnish over them. Make a list of your favorite colors so you'll remember them when you get to the store. (Dry time: 15–20 minutes.)

3-D Squeeze paint: This paint is smooth and thick, like icing. It comes in a tiny bottle with a small hole for writing. Because it's water-based, it's easy to clean up if you make a mistake. My favorite brand is Scribbles. (Dry time: At least 1 hour.)

Pens: There are special kinds of pens that can make your projects easier and better looking. You don't *really* need these (unless otherwise stated in a project), but they sure are nice to have around. **Paint pen:** A black, silver, or gold paint pen is great for outlining or adding accents. **Metallic markers:** These usually come in a packaged set for about five dollars. They work well on paper crafts such as journals, cards, and scrapbooks. **Fabric pens:** If you don't want to deal with messy paints, these ink markers make decorating clothing a zip. **Colored markers:** Um, hello? These are a definite YES! Pick up a big box of these because you can use them to doodle, write notes, and make fancy letters.

Paintbrushes

You'll need foam and/or soft-bristle brushes for base-coating and varnishing large surfaces. You'll also want very thin liner brushes for outlining and adding details. No need to buy the most expensive brushes, but don't go super-cheap, either. Keep it somewhere in between. You want your painted projects to have a nice, polished look, and that will only come from using decent brushes.

The 411 on Mixing Colors

There are a *lot* of gorgeous paint colors out there, but before you break your piggy bank to buy a bottle of every single one, take a look at these color-mixing recipes. You can make almost any color you want by simply blending the ones you already have. The only exceptions are red, blue, and yellow. These are the three "primary" colors, which means they're the only colors that can't be made by mixing other paints.

To mix a recipe, squirt equal parts of each color onto a paper plate and mix with a paintbrush. Don't waste—squeeze out only as much as you think you will use (a little goes a long way). Use these recipes as a starting point, then create even more happy hues of your own!

red **+** blue **=** purple

blue **+** yellow **=** green

yellow **+** red **=** orange

red **+** green **=** brown

green **+** yellow **=** light green

blue **+** green **=** teal

red **+** white **=** pink

blue **+** white **=** baby blue

white **+** any color **=** lighter version of that color

black **+** any color **=** darker version of that color. (Start with only a drop of the black and keep adding it, drop by drop, until you get the color you want.)

Tip Whenever you work with paint and brushes, keep a plastic tray for mixing, a small cup of water, and paper towels nearby. When you're finished painting (or to clean a brush between colors), swirl the brush in the water, pull it out, and carefully dry it off on a paper towel so the bristles don't bend.

Glitter

Glitter rocks. But you already know that. Here's the scoop on the sparkly stuff. Buy one of each—you'll need them all.

Squeeze-on glitter paint: This is just like 3-D squeeze paint, only in glittery colors. Scribbles displays its glitter paint right next to its other paint colors.

Polyester micro-fine glitter: This is a barely-there, crystal-like dust that's great for beauty recipes, like Powder-Puff Fluff on page 37.

Body glitter: This comes in a tiny jar and is water-based, kind of like a thin gel.

Fabric glitter spray: I like Tulip Permanent Fabric Glitter Spray—it comes in a small plastic spray bottle and can be used on most fabrics (but not hair or skin!) to add a sheen. (Dry time: 15–20 minutes.)

Loose glitter: This is the thick stuff that we used back in kindergarten...and still use now. Amazing, no?

Glues and Adhesives

Without glue there would be no crafting. But unlike a terrycloth wristband, one size does not fit all. Read on.

white craft glue: Almost everyone has a bottle of Elmer's glue around the house. It works fine for general crafting, and it dries clear. (Dry time: 1 hour, longer for thicker layers.)

Aleene's Original Tacky Glue: If you can only buy one kind of glue, go with this one. It's a thick and creamy, all-purpose white glue that works on most projects and dries clear. It's a fave among crafters because its thick texture prevents materials from slipping and sliding. (Dry time: 35 minutes.)

> **Tip**
> If you don't have Aleene's Original Tacky Glue on hand, you can use regular white craft glue on almost any project instead. It just might not last quite as long.

Fabric glue: Don't like sewing? Use this kind of glue to bond layers of fabric or add trims and cutout shapes. By far the best brand is Aleene's OK To Wash-It: It holds up through lots of washings, so your stuff will last much longer. (Dry time: 2 hours.)

E6000 Industrial Strength Adhesive: When Wonder Woman needs help in the adhesive department, my guess is she reaches for this silver tube. It holds metal or plastic to just about any surface, and it dries to a thick, clear, elastic substance. (Dry time: 10 minutes to "set"; a full 24 hours to "cure.")

Glue Sticks: Where would we be without them? Any brand will do—just buy a package of four, because you'll go through them pretty fast. Only for paper projects. (Dry time: 10 minutes.)

Craftfoam glue: This glue is made especially for craft foam. It's very sticky and grips the foam to prevent it from sliding. If you don't have craftfoam glue, white craft glue will work fine, too. (Dry time: 20 minutes.)

Double-sided tape: For use with lightweight paper or fabric projects.

Varnishes and Sealers

Once you finish your artistic masterpieces, you'll want to make sure they stick around for a while. If you're working with paint or decoupage, adding a final layer of varnish or sealant will protect your work from chips and scratches. There are lots of kinds to choose from, so pay close attention.

water-based varnish: This is a good all-around sealer that comes in a bottle or jar and is nontoxic and odorless. That means you can use it right in your bedroom at your craft table. There are two kinds: *gloss* and *matte*. Gloss varnish will add a high shine to your work; matte will seal your work with a dull glaze. (I'm a gloss girl myself, but it's really a matter of personal preference.) To use, apply with a brush you use just for varnishing and rinse the brush after each use. (Dry time: 30 minutes.)

Spray varnish: This varnish comes in a can, like spray paint. Any time you use a spray product you *must* wear a paper mask to keep you from breathing in any poison fumes. This means you can only use spray-on varnish outside. Not good if you're crafting on a rainy day or late at night! If you have to choose between brush-on varnish and spray varnish, go with the brush-on kind. (Dry time: 30 minutes.)

Sparkle varnish: Delta Sparkle Varnish is a high-gloss, water-based varnish that can be painted over any surface and will leave light flecks of translucent pink and blue glitter. Delta is the only brand I know that makes this kind of varnish. (Dry time: 20 minutes.)

Scissors

Mini scissors are good for getting into tight corners. Decorative scrap-booking scissors are nice for making fancy curved edges. But a brand-new pair of regular old scissors will work just fine.

Jewelry and Wire-working Tools

From wire rings to picture bracelets, there's nothing more satisfying than making your own bling-bling. That is, as long as you have the right stuff on hand.

Jump rings: When it comes to working with beads, jewelry, or dangling things, a jump ring is your new best friend. It is a small, round, metal ring used to connect one item to another. Jump rings come in a variety of sizes. For the most part, any small to medium-sized jump ring will do the trick. Pick up a pack of rings that measure anywhere from ¼ to ½ inch in diameter (or 1 to 2 cm) and you'll be all set.

Wire: Wire comes in all kinds of colors and widths. Standard wire is 24 gauge—the number tells you how thin or thick the wire is. The higher the number, the thinner the wire. The lower the number, the thicker the wire.

Needle-nose pliers: These are perfect for all kinds of crafting, such as picking up small items like beads and rhinestones and placing them on a surface. Even better, they are great with wire. Use them to twist and curl wire into any shape you like. You can also use them to cut wire, thanks to a tiny clipper built into the pliers. Best of all, most craft stores carry needle-nose pliers (as well as other wire-working and jewelry tools) made specially for girls. If you don't have a pair in the house and plan on making only one wire project, you can go without, or use tweezers instead. It will just take a bit more concentration and patience. Keep in mind that cutting wire with regular scissors will damage your scissors, so if you plan on going wire crazy, definitely pick up a set of these pliers.

Polymer Clay

It's always good to have a hunk or two of this around. There are lots of brands, but I prefer Sculpey. You can make beads with it, stamp it, paint it, and mold it. Because it requires baking and a cookie sheet, make sure you ask first for permission to use the oven, or get an adult's help.

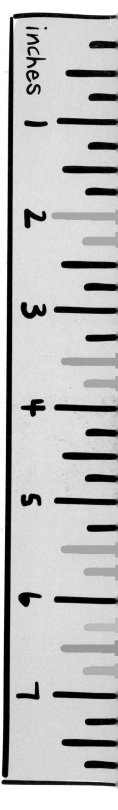

Papers, Pictures, Rubber Stamps, and Stencils

Enough with the boring stuff—papers and pictures are where it's at! These are the items that transform the ordinary into the extraordinary. Be thrifty and creative when it comes to looking for images. Wallpaper, scrap-booking paper, postcards, magazines, old schoolbooks, outdated encyclopedias, note cards, photos, stickers, and more can be found everywhere, from secondhand stores to ritzy stationery boutiques.
You can also make your own images. If you're scared to draw or write freehand, relax. This is supposed to be fun, remember? Use transfer (carbon) paper, tracing paper, or a photocopier to copy pictures from the Clip Art Treasure Chest on page 138. You can also pick up inexpensive foam stamps or stencils.

Sequins, Beads, Gems, and Rhinestones

These add a sense of elegance to anything they're glued to—well, except your retainer (that would hurt). Most craft stores offer them in huge "bulk" bags, which are way better deals than buying a bunch of small bags.

Tip

Glass beads are a bit more expensive than plastic, but the end result will be worth it! They are affordable as long as you use them sparingly.

Fabric and Clothing

Look through your closet and dresser drawers for items dying to be reworked: shirts, pants, bags, scarves, socks, shoelaces, belts, and so on. If you can't find anything super-swell, scour secondhand stores, record stores, mall boutiques, or discount department stores. And hey, see if anyone in the family has something to donate to your crafty cause!

metric (cm)

Measurement Cheat Sheet

When it comes to working with fabric, wire, and ribbon, you can usually get away with "eyeballing," or guessing, measurements. But all that changes once you've bought a yard of super far-out fabric. The last thing you'll want to do is cut it in the wrong place. So be a conscious crafter. Keep a ruler or measuring tape nearby to triple-check those digits. (Check out the built-in rulers on pages 11 and 12.) And to make things even easier (wouldn't want you to pop a blood vessel or anything), here's a cheat sheet to help you in your time of need.

in. = " = inch

ft. = ' = feet

yd. = yard

mm = millimeter

cm = centimeter

1 inch = 25 millimeters = 2.5 centimeters

1 foot = 12 inches = 30.5 centimeters

1 yard = 3 feet = 36 inches

Found Objects

Huh? These are small, weird, but very cool objects that you don't know what to do with. Old coins, postage stamps, sugar packets, small toys, game pieces, charms— they all have a place in your artistic universe. Use them to accent scrapbook or journal pages, picture frames, furniture, and more.

Sewing and Embroidery Materials

If you are brave enough to tackle sewing, you'll need a needle, thread, and straight pins. For embroidery, pick up a hoop, embroidery floss, and an embroidery needle.

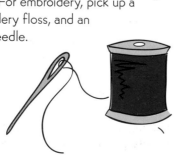

Building Your Crafty Quarters

You have all of these wonderful ideas bouncing around in your head, but no comfy place to make them come to life. Don't expect the family to give up the dining-room table—you're on your own here. What you can do is ask your parents if they'll be so kind as to buy you a twenty-dollar card table and folding chair from the discount department store. Reorganize your room and clear a corner to put the table and chair.

One rule even more serious than final exams is that you should stay organized. That means keeping things neat to avoid frustration. Group your supplies by type— glue with glue, markers with markers, glitter with glitter. Store each group in plastic baggies and put them in clear, stackable containers or shoeboxes. Slide the boxes under the table to leave your workspace free of clutter. If needed, take a permanent marker and on the outside of each box, write a list of the things inside. And always have a sketchbook and pencil nearby to keep notes and ideas.

DOs and DON'Ts

Do:

- Always check out the clearance rack for odds and ends to use in your projects.

- Take care of your materials and supplies. Treat them like they're made of gold.

- Read all instructions—twice—before starting any project.

- Respect the saying "measure twice, cut once." In other words, make *double* sure your measurements are right before you actually cut anything.

- Arrange and rearrange items to make sure you like the design before gluing them down.

- Work on one project at a time so you don't get overwhelmed.

- Sign your name on all of your finished work. It's the mark of a real artist!

- If you have a gut feeling you should ask permission from a parent before "revamping" something, ask.

- Put music on in the background. It will add to the spirit of your work.

- Remember to have fun!

Don't:

- Lend out your supplies or materials. You may not get them back!

- Leave a crafting session without putting all of your supplies away.

- Leave the lids off of glues and paints. Always replace them right away.

- Leave scissors and needles lying around. Keep them in closed containers.

- Leave paint spills for Mom to clean up, when you can do it more easily.

- Throw all of your small supplies into one bag or box. Keep them sorted and organized.

- Change anything in your house or room without asking permission first.

- Let young children around your supplies or workstation.

Whew! Enough with the chit-chat— it's time to get to work! There are so many wonderful things to glue, paint, and varnish, and so little time.

All right, you may now reach for the art smock.

Animal Lover

❋ Has at least six photos of her cat or dog in her locker, framed and covered with lipstick kisses.

❋ Likes dressing her pet in outfits that match her own...sport visor and all.

❋ Isn't sure how she feels about kissing boys, but has no problem kissing her slobbering Saint Bernard puppy.

Cats, dogs, birds, fish, and yes, even tarantulas, make lovable pets for those who adore the animal kingdom. After all, friends may come and go, but our charismatic critters will always be faithful and loyal companions. If you're an **ANIMAL LOVER**, return the love by surrounding your pets with some stylin' crafty masterpieces. You know if they could, they would do the same for you!

Paradise Pet Dish

Matching Photo Charms

Precious Pet-in-a-Jar

Paradise PET DISH

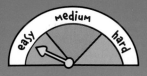

Dogs and cats loooove to be pampered. How about a steamy facial or relaxing pedicure for your pooch? Um, maybe not. Better to brighten up plain old food and water bowls into a gorgeous designer dish set. You can either buy new bowls, or just wash and dry Fido or Fifi's current set and paint away (ask Mom first). The groovy patterns will look so rad, your pet won't even notice it's the same set.

Stuff You'll Need

* plastic food and/or water bowls, clean and dry
* sharpened crayon in a light color
* 3-D squeeze paint in assorted colors
* paper
* paper towels
* water-based varnish and brush

How to Do It

1. Practice writing your pet's name in large letters on a piece of paper. Check out Doodling 101 on page 136 for ways to make the letters.

2. Using the crayon, write your pet's name on the bowl just as you practiced it on the paper. If you make a mistake, wipe away the crayon mark and try again.

3. Choose a color of the squeeze paint and trace over your crayon writing.

4. Use other colors to add swirls, zigzags, lines, and dots. If you're making a set, repeat steps 2–4 for the second bowl.

5. Let the bowl(s) dry overnight, then brush on a coat of varnish to seal in your hard work.

Tip

Squeeze paint is neat stuff. If you mess up, carefully wipe it off with a paper towel and start over. Sometimes the tip of the bottle will clog. If this happens, don't scream! Just keep a safety pin close by so you can pop off the top of the container and poke the pin through the hole to remove any gunk. Put the top back on and go back to squeezing.

Other Ideas

❀ Use letter stencils if you don't want to "freehand" the name.

❀ Use a ceramic bowl and Delta Perm Enamel glass paint for a more artsy look. (Be ready to shell out some extra change, though.)

❀ Ditch the paints altogether and use colorful stickers to decorate your pet's dish. Don't forget to varnish it so your stickers will stay put.

Matching PHOTO CHARMS

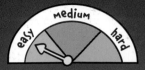

Some may say you love your pet a tad too much. Now why would they say that, just because you can't leave the house without crying on its shoulder and giving it two minutes of kisses? That's true love! Because breaking up is so hard to do, here's a way for the two of you to remember each other until you're reunited.

Stuff You'll Need

- ❈ 2 small photos of you
- ❈ 2 small photos of your pet
- ❈ package of self-laminating sheets (found in office supply or craft stores)
- ❈ 1 quarter
- ❈ pen or pencil
- ❈ 2 jump rings
- ❈ 2 large lobster-claw clasps (optional)
- ❈ Aleene's Original Tacky Glue
- ❈ hole puncher
- ❈ scissors
- ❈ key ring

How to Do It

1. Take one of the photos and place it so the face is centered on the quarter. Hold it still with your finger and flip it over, setting it on the table. Trace around the quarter, then cut around the outline. Do the same with the other photos.

2. Take one photo of your pet and one of you and glue them together, back to back. Make sure the tops of your heads face the same way so they will hang right. Let dry. Repeat for the other two photos.

3. Remove one laminating sheet from the package. Open the two plastic flaps that are connected at one side. Peel off the backing so the sticky side is exposed and place the double-sided photos on the sticky surface. Bring the other flap down over the photos and smooth it out with your fingers. Lamination is now complete.

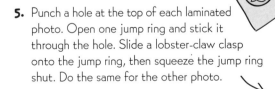

4. Cut around the edge of each photo, leaving a thin border. Do not cut too close to the photo's edge or the lamination will come apart.

5. Punch a hole at the top of each laminated photo. Open one jump ring and stick it through the hole. Slide a lobster-claw clasp onto the jump ring, then squeeze the jump ring shut. Do the same for the other photo.

6. Attach one photo charm to your pet's collar. Attach the other one to a key ring for you. (If you don't have lobster-claw clasps, attach the jump rings directly to the collar and key ring.)

Other Ideas

- ❈ Make several photo charms for use as a bracelet, necklace, or in a scrap-booking project.

Precious PET-IN-A-JAR

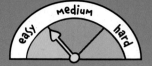

Have you ever wanted a pet giraffe or rhino, but knew your parents would freak? There's no need to throw a temper tantrum, you can still have the pet of your choice right in your bedroom. Well, at least in miniature size. And that's better than nothing, wouldn't you say?

Stuff You'll Need

* empty glass jar with lid, clean and dry, with label removed
* small plastic toy animal (found at the party store)
* loose glitter
* mini metallic stars in assorted colors (optional)
* light corn syrup (optional)
* E6000 glue
* scissors
* ribbon

How to Do It

1. Place your toy upside down inside the jar. Trim its legs or ears with the scissors if it's a little too big.

2. Fill the jar almost to the top with water. Add a tiny drop of the corn syrup. Add a small handful of glitter and/or stars to the water.

3. Put a tiny bit of E6000 glue onto a paper towel and rub it around the inside lip of the jar's lid. This is so it will stay put on the jar. Put the lid on and twist it shut, making sure the grooves are lined up straight.

4. Turn the jar upside down and shake. If it leaks, flip it over and reattach the lid, then try again.

5. Add a small line of glue around the outside of the lid and press on a piece of ribbon. Your lovely new pet is now free to roam about the jar as he or she pleases!

Other Ideas

* Make a glittery zoo by creating lots of jars and displaying them together. Or use a larger jar and put more than one animal inside.

Tip

An empty baby-food jar is the perfect size container for this project. You could also use an empty mustard jar, jam jar, or any small-sized glass jar. Remove the label by running the jar under warm water, then use a dish scrubber to get rid of any stubborn glue.

* Curls up with not only one good book, but two or three.

* Works on homework for her English class, even when there isn't any.

* Plans on publishing her first novel by the time she finishes high school.

While everyone else is wasting away the hours at the school basketball game, or window-shopping at the mall, the ARTFUL BOOKWORM is all about peace and quiet. Whether that sigh of delight comes from reading a book or doodling in one, time spent alone soaking up a few pages puts your imagination into fantasy overdrive. Here are some ideas to motivate your spirit.

Magnificent Magnetic Poetry

Dimensional Diary

Beaded Bookmarks

Magnificent MAGNETIC POETRY

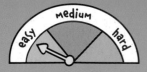

Magnetic poetry is so addictive. All the words are there, jumbled up in that little box, just waiting for someone to string them together in a kooky sentence. But instead of buying a bunch of words someone else thought were interesting, why not exercise your wordy talents to make up your own set?

Stuff You'll Need

* small box to paint and/or decorate
* craft acrylic paint and paintbrush
* things to decorate your box (trim, gems, sequins, and so on)
* white craft glue
* paper and pencil
* scissors
* package of magnet sheets for use in an Inkjet computer
* computer with word-processing program (optional)

How to Do It

1. Paint your box and let dry. Use the white craft glue to attach sequins or trim as decoration.

2. Take the paper and pencil and jot down a list of your favorite words, phrases, names, and letters. Think of people in your life, foods, flavors, places, activities, gross or really cool things, action words, and funny sayings. You'll be creating sentences, so don't forget word endings and little connecting words, like "es, ed, ing, a, an, the, and, it, it's," and so on. Oh! And don't forget punctuation marks, like periods, commas, and exclamation points. Don't freak, but it might be a good idea to flip through your school grammar book for ideas.

3. Using your computer's word-processing program, type in your words and marks, leaving two spaces between each one. Continue until you reach the end of the page.

4. Print out a sample sheet of your words and "proof" it by reading it over super closely to look for mistakes. If you find any, go back and fix them in the computer.

5. Insert the magnet sheet into the printer. (Follow the directions on your printer so you know which way to feed the sheet, faceup or facedown. Most are faceup.) Print.

6. Remove the sheet from the printer and cut the tiny words apart. Put them in your decorated box. Now you can use them on a locker, fridge, or magnet board.

Tip If you don't have a computer, use a fine-point permanent marker to handwrite the words on the magnetic sheet instead.

Dimensional DIARY

Diaries are great for recording your secret thoughts, and scrapbooks are awesome for photos and other mementos. When you combine the two, you have an art journal that's a whole new level of expressing yourself. This type of journal is also known as an "altered book" because you take an old book and "alter" the pages. Look for old books in thrift stores, flea markets, and yard sales—best is a hardcover book with lots of colorful pictures.

Stuff You'll Need

* hardcover book that you don't mind writing and painting on
* pictures of friends
* magazines you can cut up
* watercolor paints and paintbrush
* trimmings like sequins, fabric trims, rhinestones, and feathers
* metallic and ballpoint pens
* stickers
* glue stick
* scissors

How to Do It

1. Start by looking through the book for a spread (two facing pages) just screaming to be revamped.

2. Use your watercolor paints and brush to add a light layer of color onto the pages, either in one area or over the whole spread. Let dry.

3. Use the glue stick to add photos of friends, and pictures and words you cut out from magazines. Use the metallic pens to doodle on the book's pictures. Look for an empty-ish area where you can jot down notes, memories, poems, or stories. Add sequins, trims, rhinestones, and feathers. Leave the spread open until all your work dries.

4. Continue to fill up your diary by doing other pages. Always leave a few empty pages in between decorated spreads.

5. Don't forget to decorate the cover of your book!

Tip

Stick with thin, lightweight objects. After decorating all those pages, your book won't close flat, but that's a good thing. That means you have lots of memories to look back on!

Beaded BOOKMARKS

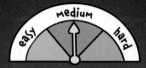

Stop! Don't even think of folding over the corner of that page, especially if it's a nail-biting, can't-wait-to-see-what-happens-next, page-turner kind of book. Why damage it forever when you can make a super-fantastico bookmark to keep your place instead? Take a seat at your craft table, close your eyes, and let your excitement for that book flow through your bod and out your fingertips. The sooner you finish making one of these brilliant bookmarks, the sooner you can get back to reading.

Stuff You'll Need

- ★ sheet of card stock or thick cardboard
- ★ assorted pieces of fabric or decorative paper
- ★ embroidery floss or thin ribbon in various colors
- ★ medium-sized beads with large holes
- ★ small silver grommets (2 per bookmark) (optional)

- ★ jump rings (2 per bookmark) (optional)
- ★ eye pins (1 or 2 per bookmark) (optional)
- ★ needle-nose pliers (only if using eye pins)
- ★ hole puncher
- ★ tracing paper (optional)
- ★ ruler (optional)
- ★ glue stick
- ★ scissors

Tip Grommets are small rings used in scrap-booking that are smooth on one side and have "teeth" on the other. You can find them in any craft or scrap-booking store. They'll give your bookmarks a fancy, polished look. If you don't have grommets, don't worry—you can still make the bookmarks without them.

How to Do It

1. Trace the template on the facing page onto tracing paper and cut around the outline. Then use the template to cut bookmark shapes out of the card stock or thick cardboard. (Or just use a ruler to draw rectangles measuring 2 × 6 inches on the card stock, then cut them out.)

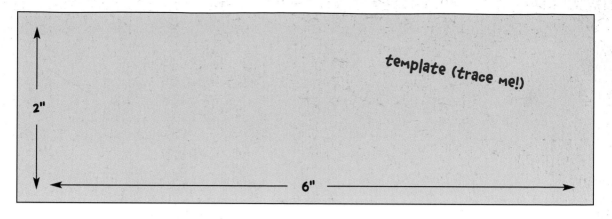

2"

6"

template (trace me!)

2. Lay the fabric or paper facedown on a table. Take one of the bookmarks and rub the glue stick over one side, from edge to edge. Press onto the fabric or paper. Rub your fingers over it to smooth out any bumps. Repeat the process with the rest of the bookmarks. Let dry for 20 minutes, then cut them out, trimming off the extra fabric or paper.

Tip

Don't use liquid glue on this project— it will make your bookmarks come out lumpy and wavy.

3. Repeat step 2 to cover the other side of the bookmarks.

4. Decide which end of each bookmark you want to be the top. Use the hole puncher to punch a hole ½ inch down from that end. Press a grommet through the hole, then press the grommet's "teeth" in place from behind.

5. Open a jump ring and slide it through the grommet, then squeeze the jump ring shut with your fingers.

6. Place a couple beads on an eye pin. Loop the end through the jump ring and bend it closed using the needle-nose pliers.

Tip

Don't have grommets, jump rings, or eye pins? Forget about 'em. Just thread a strand of floss or ribbon through the hole you made with the punch and make a knot to secure it. String some beads onto the ribbon and make another knot at the end to hold the beads in place.

7. Punch a hole at the other end of each bookmark. Put a grommet in the hole, as you did before, and attach another jump ring. Thread the ribbon or floss through the jump ring and tie it with a knot to secure it. Let the strands hang about 6 inches and trim off the rest. (If you aren't using grommets or jump rings, just thread the ribbon or floss through the hole you punched.)

8. When you use your bookmark, place it in your book so the beads hang out over the top of the page and the ribbon hangs out the bottom.

Other Ideas

★ Cut your bookmarks out of white watercolor paper, then use watercolor paints to add designs.

Beautiful Bohemian

* IS one with the universe.

* Stops in delight whenever she sees a rainbow.

* Sees herself as a flower child of the '60s, just born a little too late.

The BEAUTIFUL BOHEMIAN doesn't care about the latest entertainment magazines, TV shows, or Top 40 hits— she'd rather spend quality time doing something to change the world. Bohemians are happy people who are dreamy, free-spirited, and very artsy-crafty. They love to have fun, and to bring out the best in others. In other words, they add a cheery rainbow to cloudy days. If this sounds like you, these whimsical projects will make you smile even more!

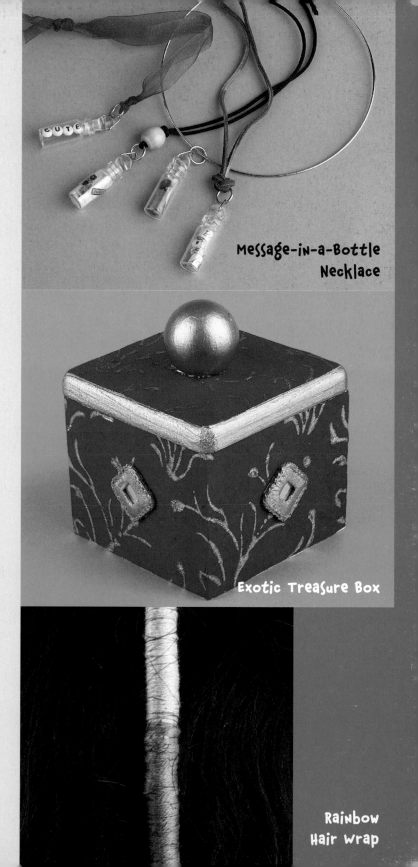

Message-in-a-Bottle Necklace

Exotic Treasure Box

Rainbow Hair Wrap

Message-in-a-Bottle NECKLACE

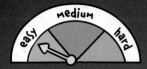

Falling stars are great to wish on, but they aren't exactly easy to find on a day-to-day basis. Instead, make this adorable little bottle necklace that's the perfect place to tuck away your private inspirations. Mini bottles are easy to find at scrapbook and craft stores.

Stuff You'll Need

* mini glass bottle with removable top
* tiny things to place inside your bottle
* ribbon or thin leather strip, 16 inches long
* jump ring
* toothpick
* scissors

How to Do It

1. Decide what to put inside your bottle. Any items that are paper or fabric can be trimmed with the scissors to fit inside. If using tiny notes, write your words on small, thin strips of paper and roll them tightly so you can just pop them inside the bottle.

Tip Can't think of what to put in your bottle? Here are some ideas: letter beads that spell a secret name or word, loose glitter, mini notes, fabric flowers, or colored beads.

2. Stick the toothpick inside the bottle's opening and move the items around to your liking.

3. Put the top back on the bottle. Make sure it fits snugly. If it's loose, you may have to remove some of the items. The last thing you want is for the top to come flying off during gym class!

4. Bend open the jump ring and attach it to the top of the bottle, through its wire loop. Bend the jump ring shut.

5. Thread the ribbon or leather strip through the jump ring and bring the ends up so they meet evenly. Tie them together in a strong knot.

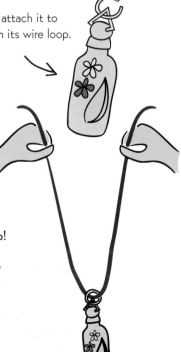

Other Ideas

* These little bottles are cheap! Grab a handful to make one for every day of the week, or swap them with your favorite gal pals.

Exotic TREASURE BOX

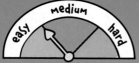

One of the perks of having an airy bohemian personality is that you will someday (if you haven't already) travel the world to experience other cultures. But don't wait until then to treat yourself to exotic treasures from other lands. This decorated wooden box is so spectacular you'll want to make more for holiday or birthday gifts.

Stuff You'll Need

- small- or medium-sized wooden box with lid
- piece of fabric or paper, 24 x 12 inches
- craft acrylic paint that matches your fabric or paper, and paintbrush
- wooden ball (optional)
- decorative mirrors (optional)
- white craft glue, paper plate, and foam brush
- E6000 glue
- ruler
- scissors

How to Do It

1. Paint the inside of the box, the wooden ball, and the edge of the lid. Let dry.

2. Lay the fabric facedown on the table. Squeeze some white craft glue onto the paper plate. Dip the foam brush into the glue and spread it thinly and evenly across each side of the box, from edge to edge. When they are all covered with glue, pick up the box from the inside and place it along the edge of the fabric. Press firmly.

3. Hold the box and slowly turn it so the next side is against the fabric. Press it in place. Repeat until all four sides of the box are covered.

4. Slide the fabric so that its edge lines up with the edge of the box. Rub it to smooth out any bubbles. Trim off extra fabric. Set aside.

5. Lay the remaining fabric facedown on the table. Paint a layer of white glue on the top of the lid and press it firmly onto the fabric. Lift it up, smooth it out, and trim off the extra.

6. Apply a drop of E6000 glue to the bottom of the wooden ball and set in the middle of the lid. Let dry. Then apply a drop of glue to the back of each mirror and press in place, one on each side.

Other Ideas

- Cut up fancy gift wrap and magazines and make a collage-covered box. Use white craft glue to apply one piece at a time to the box until the entire surface is covered. Let dry, then seal it by brushing on a layer of water-based varnish.

Rainbow HAIR WRAP

Forget about hair gel, styling spray, and trendy barrettes. You want something more earthy and colorful that doesn't just go on top of your hair, but around it. These rainbow hair wraps are soooo it. They're fun to put together because it takes two to tango—invite a friend to join. The idea is to take turns wrapping strands of each other's hair. While you're working, you can be chatting about ways to recycle, save the rain forest, or make your favorite veggie burgers.

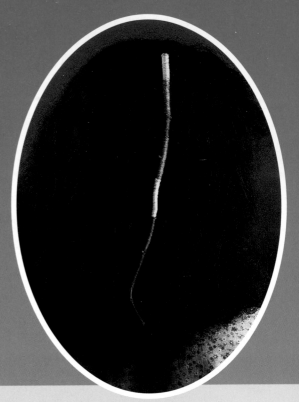

Stuff You'll Need

* hairbrush
* embroidery floss in assorted colors
* small ponytail holder
* scissors

How to Do It

1. Start with whatever color of floss you want to have on the top of the hair wrap. Remove the label and find the floss end on the *inside* of the roll. Don't use the end on top of the roll because when you pull it, the entire roll will tangle and that will make you very angry.

2. Brush the hair where you are going to apply the wrap. Pull aside a small strand of hair (about the thickness of a pencil). Hold it from the top. Take the end of the floss and hold it in place at the top of the hair.

3. Using your other hand, wrap the floss around the hair one time. Tie the two pieces of floss in a knot.

4. Begin to tightly wrap the floss around the strand of hair. Continue until you have 1 inch of the hair wrapped. Snip off the extra floss, leaving a short tail hanging down.

Words of Wisdom

There's more than just the "normal" way to do things and see life—once you realize that, you'll be amazed at the creative ideas you start coming up with.

—Leticia de la Vara, 26, musician and clothing designer

Take little breaks in between colors to shake out your arms so they don't fall asleep.

Tip

5. Switch colors and find the end of the new color. Starting where you left off, hold the end of the new color at the base of the last color. Use your other hand to wrap the new color around the old color once to keep the old color in place. Then tie the new color to the tail from the old color, making a knot. Continue to wrap for another inch.

6. Keep using different colors all the way down, wrapping each color for about 1 inch. When you reach the end of the hair, pinch the floss around the strand. Use your other hand to snip off the floss, leaving a tail, then put a ponytail holder over the end of the wrap to secure it. Snip off any extra floss. To remove the wrap, just snip off the knot and unravel.

Other Ideas

✹ Use color schemes from your school or favorite sports team.

✹ This is a fun party activity—have a contest to see who can wrap the fastest and neatest.

✹ Use this same method to decorate a disposable pen. When you're done wrapping, put a dab of white glue on the end of the floss to seal it.

7. Hand over the floss and scissors to your friend so she can add a rainbow wrap to your hair!

- Always adds a dash of body glitter to her eyelids...and to everyone else's, too.

- Cruises the makeup aisle at the grocery store as a form of entertainment.

- Considers herself a true woman of science—the science of beauty, that is.

Have you ever loved the fruity smell of one shampoo, but the silky feeling of another? The BEAUTY CHEMIST never worries about which beauty product to use. She simply mixes and matches them to create her own perfect blend. That talent is one of the perks of being a beauty chemist. Not to mention it's also tons of fun. Especially when you get to mix up body-licious recipes like these to make your inside and outside glow.

Glamorous Glitter Gloss

Bubblegum Soap Bars

Powder-Puff Fluff

Glamorous GLITTER GLOSS

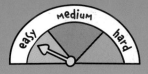

With so many choices of gloss at the store, a girl can empty her piggy bank in no time. Here's a cheap and speedy way to make your own tinted lip gloss from ingredients you probably already have around the house.

Stuff You'll Need

- o small empty container with screw-on lid
- o craft acrylic paints and paintbrush
- o things to decorate the jar (gems, beads, or glass pebbles)
- o petroleum jelly (like Vaseline)
- o your favorite color lipstick
- o body glitter gel
- o white craft glue
- o chopstick or toothpick
- o plastic knife or bread knife
- o paper plate

How to Do It

1. Start by preparing your container. (Small containers can be bought cheaply at the craft store. You can also ask your mom or sis if they have any to donate to the crafty cause.) Remove the lid and wash both parts thoroughly in warm, soapy water. Let dry.

2. Paint the top of the container lid with either a solid color or a design and let dry. Use the glue to add a gem, glass pebble, or lots of tiny beads on top of the paint. Let dry.

3. Use the knife to remove a small glob of petroleum jelly and place it inside the container. Make sure the container gets only half full.

4. Open the lipstick over the paper plate and, ever so gently, scrape off a thin slice of it onto the plate. Place the slice inside the container with the jelly. Stir with the chopstick or toothpick until all the color is blended into the jelly.

5. Add a dash of the body glitter and mix again. Screw the lid on tightly.

Other Ideas

O Add a tiny sliver of flavored lip balm for taste.

O Design a label for your glitter gloss on a sticker and press onto the container. Congratulations, you're an official beauty chemist!

POWDER-PUFF Fluff

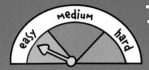

What better way to start or end the day than with a sprinkling of sparkly body dust? This homemade body powder, or powder-puff fluff as we like to call it, will make after-bath time mucho fun. There's just something about that micro glitter that makes us feel all tingly inside.

Tip

Body powder, body glitter, powder puffs, and/or soft body brushes can be found at bath and beauty stores as well as lots of drugstores. Empty jars can be recycled from the kitchen, or bought at a craft or dollar store.

Stuff You'll Need

- large empty jar with screw-on lid
- things to decorate the jar (gems, stickers, sequins, paint, fabric, and/or ribbon)
- white craft glue (if needed)
- Polyester ultra-fine loose body glitter, crystal-white color
- white body powder (perfumed, if you like)
- plastic bowl
- mixing spoon
- powder puff or soft body brush

How to Do It

1. Wash and thoroughly dry the empty jar. Decorate the jar and lid with stickers (like the one shown here) or use white craft glue to apply gems, fabric, sequins, and/or ribbons. Let dry.

2. Carefully pour about 1 cup of body powder into the plastic bowl. Add 3 pinches of the ultra-fine body glitter to the bowl. Slowly (so it doesn't poof up into the air and make you sneeze), mix the powder and glitter together with the spoon. Hello powder-puff fluff!

3. Gently spoon the fairy dust into the jar until it's full. Screw the lid back on tightly.

4. Apply your sparkly powder with the puff or soft body brush after you dry off from the shower or bath. Dab it on your arms, neck, legs, even behind your ears. Because it's all jazzed up, keep it out on the counter for others to see.

Other Ideas

- Double the batch to make a nice gift for a friend or to leave at Grandma's house after a weekend visit.

Bubblegum SOAP BARS

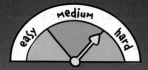

The party at your place is all planned and ready to go. Except for one thing: gifts for your guests. You could easily pick up some cheesy plastic horns (yawn...so predictable), or you could spend a few hours making a batch of these cool pink bubblegum soap bars. They're your friends, you choose which way to go. By the way, all of the soap-making supplies, like the base and the fragrance, can be found at your local craft store.

Ouch! Melt-and-pour soap is very hot and can seriously burn your skin if you're not paying close attention. So read these instructions with a parent or other adult before even *thinking* of starting this project. Got it, missy? You and your friends will be so glad you did.

Stuff You'll Need

- white melt-and-pour soap base, 2-pound package
- bubblegum scented skin-safe soap fragrance
- pink soap coloring
- rectangular-shaped soap mold, or any plastic container that holds 2 pounds of liquid
- wax paper or paper towels
- knife
- glass measuring cup
- pot holders
- plastic spoon or set of chopsticks
- tablespoon
- microwave oven
- clear plastic wrap
- cute fabric (optional)
- pink ribbon (optional)

How to Do It

1. Line your work area with paper towels or wax paper. Have an adult cut the melt-and-pour soap base into 1-inch square chunks.

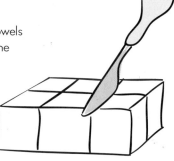

2. Place your chunks into the glass measuring cup. Put in the microwave on high for 30 seconds, then check to see if it's all melted. Repeat until all of the squares are melted. It should look like a creamy white soup.

3. Using the pot holders, place the glass measuring cup on the counter. Add the coloring a few drops at a time until you get the shade you like. The more drops you add, the darker your soap will be. Carefully (so you don't spill or splash) stir the melted soap with the spoon or chopsticks until the color is blended.

Ouch!

Okay, one more reminder. Please use extreme caution when handling melted soap as it can get *very* hot. If the melted soap is boiling or bubbling when you open the microwave, leave it in there for a few minutes until the bubbling stops.

4. Pour in 2 tablespoons of the bubblegum fragrance. Carefully mix it thoroughly with the spoon or chopsticks.

5. Pour the melted soap into the mold or plastic container, filling it almost to the top. Let it cool for 2 hours.

6. Turn the mold or container over and carefully twist it until a long soap "log" pops out. Have an adult cut 1-inch slices from the log. This will make 10 to 12 bars of bubblegum soap.

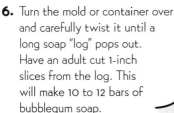
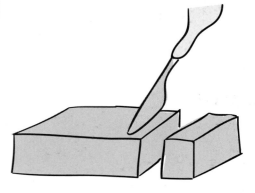

7. Wrap each bar in cellophane, clear plastic wrap, or pieces of fabric. Tie each with pink ribbon.

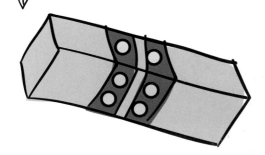

Other Ideas

○ Cut each bar into 1-inch squares to look like real pieces of bubble gum!

○ Wrap each piece of soap in wax paper and twist the ends to look like bubblegum wrappers, or create your own personalized wrapper using a computer. Just be sure you tell people it's really soap before you give them a piece!

Drama
Queen

- ⊚ Throws heart-wrenching hissy fits at least once a week.

- ⊚ Is able to cry on demand.

- ⊚ Turns a simple "hi" into an award-worthy melodramatic moment ("HELLOOOOO Sweetie! You look FAB-O! New hairdo? It works for you!").

Happiness, sadness, joy, anger—every girl has her range of emotions. But while most of us tend to stay somewhere in the middle, the DRAMA QUEEN likes to cover them all—on an hourly basis. She also happens to have a killer eye roll and is **not** afraid to use it. There's only one way to appease you dramatic types, and that's to politely send you to the crafting table where you can pour all that emotion into something creative.

ROCK STAR
BASKETBALL
CHICKEN FINGER
Two Weeks Notice

Mystery Mask

Mega Mosaic Mirror

CHARADES-in-a-Can

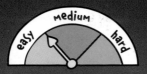

Drama queens are really just actresses in training. And what better way to sharpen those skills than with a good game of charades? This easy-to-make game fits snugly into a can, so you can take it from party to party. And on days when there is nothing (gasp!) to overreact about, you can use it to practice with.

Stuff You'll Need

- can with lid, tall enough to hold the sticks (an empty coffee can is perfect!)
- craft acrylic paints and paintbrush
- metallic or black fine-point permanent marker
- 5 index cards
- 25 tongue depressors or Popsicle sticks
- wrapping paper
- white craft glue
- 2 glue sticks
- paper and pencil
- scissors
- wooden ball or gem (optional)

How to Do It

1. Take your five index cards and write one of these categories on each: Movies, Music, Food, Things, People. Now take your paper and pencil and write down five things for each category. For example, your five foods might be popcorn, hamburger, ice cream, apple, and cookie. Your five people might be movie star, doctor, rock star, babysitter, and baseball player (or use actual names, like Marilyn Monroe or Santa Claus).

2. Divide your 25 sticks into five groups. There should be five sticks in each group. Paint each group of sticks a different color. For example, you could have five purple sticks, five red sticks, five yellow sticks, and so on. Let everything dry.

3. Place the wrapping paper facedown on the table. Cover one side of one stick with white craft glue. Press the stick firmly onto the wrapping paper so it sets. Repeat for all 25 sticks. Let dry for several minutes.

4. Cut the paper from around the sticks and throw the extra paper away. Now sort the sticks by color back into their five groups. Take your five index cards and put one card with each group. For example, the movie card with the purple sticks, the food card with the red sticks, and so on. Mark each card with an "x" in the color of its group.

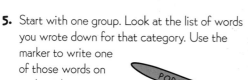

5. Start with one group. Look at the list of words you wrote down for that category. Use the marker to write one of those words on each stick. Do the same for each of the other groups.

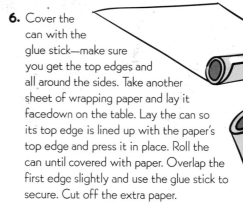

6. Cover the can with the glue stick—make sure you get the top edges and all around the sides. Take another sheet of wrapping paper and lay it facedown on the table. Lay the can so its top edge is lined up with the paper's top edge and press it in place. Roll the can until covered with paper. Overlap the first edge slightly and use the glue stick to secure. Cut off the extra paper.

7. Cover the top of the can's lid with more paper, or paint on designs. Let dry. Finish the top by gluing a painted wooden ball or gem onto the center. Let dry.

8. Put the sticks in the can, close the lid, and you're ready to roll!

Other Ideas

● Try a movie edition with categories like drama, comedy, action, romance, and cartoons. Like to groove? Make a music edition with categories like rock, pop, hip-hop, soul, and country. Get the idea?

How to Play Charades

Charades is a crazy party game in which each person takes turns acting out different things. It's also a hilarious way to see how well you can communicate—without saying a word! Here's how to play.

1. Have one person watch the clock because each turn is only one minute long. Have another person keep score. Divide the crowd into two teams.

2. You go first so you can show everyone how to play. Stand in front of the crowd. Have someone hold the five index cards out to you, facedown. Pick one. That is the category for your turn. Show everyone the index card so they can see the category, too.

3. Look at the color on the index card. Pull a stick of that same color from the can and look at its word, not letting anyone else see it. Set the stick word-side down someplace. Have the clock-watcher say "GO!"—you have one minute to act out the word to your team without talking. Your team yells out guesses as you go. If someone gets it right, your team gets a point. If time runs out and no one's gotten it right, the other team gets *one* guess. If it's right, they get a point.

4. Now it's the other team's turn, with one person choosing a category and picking a different stick. Keep playing until everyone on both teams has had a turn or you run out of sticks. If you're having a big party, make more sticks.

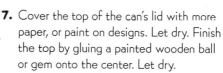

Mystery MASK

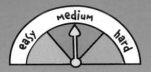

Masks are marvelous. From the slick black one that Catwoman wears to the frilly ones at old-fashioned masquerade balls, they make the wearer look ever-so-mysterious. Try this mask on for size and keep it handy for when you don't want to be recognized at the dinner table.

Stuff You'll Need

- piece of thick, colored Fun Foam or cardboard
- 3-D squeeze paint in assorted colors
- craft acrylic paints and paintbrush
- assorted sequins and rhinestones
- mini flower buds (optional)
- E6000 glue
- chopstick or other kind of stick
- tracing paper and pencil
- scissors

How to Do It

1. Lay the tracing paper over the mask template on page 141. Trace the outline and the eyeholes with the pencil. Cut out your shape (and the eyeholes).

2. Lay the tracing-paper pattern on top of the Fun Foam or cardboard. Outline the shape and the eyeholes with the pencil. Cut out the mask (including the eyeholes).

3. Decorate the front of the mask with painted designs. Put dots of 3-D squeeze paint all over it and put sequins on top of the dots. (The paint will act as glue to hold them in place.) Do the same to add rhinestones and

mini flower buds. Set aside. Take the stick and paint it in a color that matches the mask. Let everything dry for several hours.

4. Flip the mask over and put a glob of E6000 glue on one side. Place your stick on top of the glue and hold it in place for several minutes until it sets. Do not use your mask until the glue has completely dried (overnight is best).

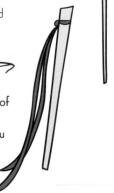

Other Ideas

- For even more drama, tie long strands of colored ribbon to the top of the stick so they hang down. (Do this before you glue the stick to the mask.)

Mega MOSAIC MIRROR

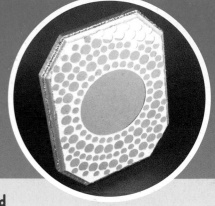

Dah-ling, you are simply divine. That angelic face of yours has the cutest boy in your homeroom quivering with adoration (though he does a good job of hiding it). For this reason, no ordinary mirror will do. You need one that shows fifty different angles to make sure every part of your smiling mug is perfect. Have no fear, the mega mosaic mirror is here! By the way, mini mirrors and grout can be found at your local craft store.

Stuff You'll Need

- flat piece of wood, 9 x 12 x 1 inches
- 1 mirror, 4 inches in diameter (from left to right edge)
- 6 packages of mini mirrors, each 1 inch in diameter
- 6 packages of mini mirrors, each ½ inch in diameter
- premixed grout
- craft acrylic paint and paintbrush
- E6000 glue
- sponge
- paper towels
- Popsicle stick or plastic knife
- plastic gloves
- sawtooth picture hanger

How to Do It

1. Paint the edges of the wood. Let dry.

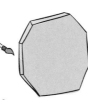

2. Add a drop of E6000 glue to the back of the large mirror and press it firmly onto the center of the wood.

3. Arrange the mini mirrors around the larger mirror in any pattern you like. Pick up one at a time and put a small drop of glue on the back, then set it back in place. Keep doing this until all of the mirrors are glued down. Let dry overnight.

4. Cover your workspace with newspaper and put on the plastic gloves. Scoop out a glob of grout with the Popsicle stick and put it onto the mirrors. Glide the grout over and into the spaces between the mirrors. Some areas may be tricky—you might have to push the grout in with your fingers. Keep going until all the spaces are filled to the same level as the mirrors. If you get grout on your clothes, the floor, or your little brother, just scrub it off with a damp cloth.

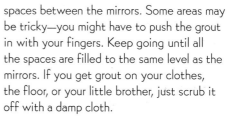

5. Dampen the sponge, then use it to wipe off any extra grout. Rinse out the sponge and wipe the surface again until there is only a faint "haze" over the mirrors. Let dry overnight.

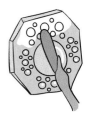

6. Use the paper towel to wipe each mirror until it's clear and shiny. Put two thick globs of E6000 on the back of the sawtooth picture hanger and press it onto the mirror's back. Gently lay the mirror facedown and let dry overnight.

Hey! Be safe! Never, ever break mirrors to make them smaller. Only use mini mirrors purchased from craft stores. They have sealed, smooth edges.

Faithful Friend

* Can work three-way calling with her hands tied behind her back.

* Always has a bag packed and ready to go for last-minute sleepover invitations.

* Starts filling out Valentine's Day cards the week after New Year's.

What's more important than having an awesome pal near-by? The FAITHFUL FRIEND never has to look far to find her best buds—they stick by her side because they know she's got their backs 24/7. She loves to make people happy, even if it means making something really neat and then giving it away. If you're a friend 'til the end, here are some nifty knickknacks you can make and share with your favorite gal (and guy) pals.

Scrabble Photo Magnets

Stamped Sticker Sheets

Tin Time Capsules

Scrabble PHOTO MAGNETS

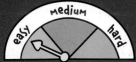

Magnets show off the things that make us smile. You know, like ultra-cute pictures of boys and funny phrases. The best thing about magnets is that you can make them out of anything. Well, almost anything. Oatmeal and french fries won't work, but old game and puzzle pieces will. Try these on for size, then think of other small, weird items to use. Just make sure you ask permission before gluing away.

Stuff You'll Need

* unwanted Scrabble game pieces
* mini photos of friends (the tiny pictures on the proof sheet that comes with your processed film are the perfect size!)
* magnets with adhesive backs (sticky backs with peel-off tape)
* white craft glue
* scissors
* water-based varnish and small brush

How to Do It

1. Cut out the tiny photos. It works best to use one picture per game piece.

2. Put a small drop of glue on the back of one photo. Spread it with your finger so the whole area is covered. Wipe your finger clean.

3. Quickly place the photo on the plain side of the game piece. Press it down and smooth out any bubbles. Let dry. Repeat with the other photos and game pieces.

4. Brush a coat of varnish over each tile and let dry.

5. Take the magnet, peel off the back to expose the sticky side, and press it onto the back of the tile.

Other Ideas

* Make chunky glass magnets using flat glass pebbles, which you can find in your local pet store (in the fish department) or craft store (in the floral department). Cut out favorite pictures and words. Put a drop of white craft glue on the *front* of each cutout and press it to the back of a pebble, so the word or image shows through the glass. Trim any paper that goes past the edge. Let dry, then attach a magnet to the back.

Stamped STICKER Sheets

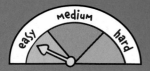

Stickers come in so many fantastic designs, it's no wonder we love to collect them. Here's a way to make a designer sticker set of your own. Any grocery store or office supply store has all kinds of blank stickers. Pick up a pack and draw away! Make them to give as gifts—your friends will love that you took the time to add a handmade touch. Okay, go ahead and make some for yourself, too.

Stuff You'll Need

* package of blank sticker sheets in any size, shape, or color
* watercolor paints and paintbrush
* rubber stamps and inkpads
* metallic and colored markers, colored pens and pencils, and gel or glitter pens
* scissors

How to Do It

1. Dip your paintbrush into a cup of water and then in the watercolor paint of your choice. Take one sheet of the stickers and lightly run your brush across the top. You can either paint the entire sheet in one color or add other colors. Try painting each sticker with strokes of different shades; just make sure to rinse your brush between colors so they don't blend into an icky brown. Watercolors dry very fast—you only have a couple minutes if you want to blend colors. Let dry.

2. Now it's time to go crazy and decorate away. Use rubber stamps, markers, or pencils to doodle all over the stickers. Write your friends' names or draw designs. Be creative! (Don't forget to check out Doodling 101 on page 136, and the Clip Art Treasure Chest on page 138.) If you goof on one sticker, just let it go and move on to the next one.

3. Cut the stickers apart, or give them away one sheet at a time.

Other Ideas

* Cut out words, letters, or pictures from magazines and use a glue stick to apply them to the blank stickers.
* Make a batch of stickers to label your craft supply boxes or notebooks.

Tin TIME CAPSULES

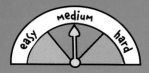

Scrapbooks and photo albums are fun ways to show off your all-time favorite pictures and memories. But why not try something a little different? Here's an artsy alternative that's made from something you probably already have lying around: mint tins. These pint-sized metal boxes are just screaming to be painted and covered with shiny goodies. And the inside is roomy enough to keep secret treasures and photos of friends. Mint tins are so easy to come by, you can make a time capsule for each month of the year and give them to friends on their birthdays, holidays, or, well, any day at all!

Stuff You'll Need

* empty mint tin with connected lid
* small mementos of friendships, like photos, ticket stubs, and notes
* scraps of decorative paper or gift wrap
* clippings of words from magazines or comics
* craft acrylic paint and paintbrush
* paint pens
* white craft glue
* medium-grade sandpaper
* water-based varnish and brush

How to Do It

1. Wash the mint tin with warm, soapy water. Let dry completely.

2. Open the tin and rub the entire outside surface with sandpaper to remove the paint. You don't have to take all of it off, but try to get most of it. This will help your paint grip better. Wipe off any dust.

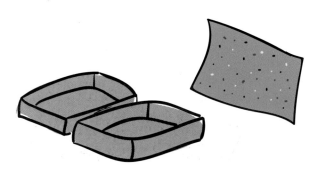

3. Close the tin's lid (if you paint with the lid open, it won't close when you're done). Paint the sides of the tin, holding it at the top and bottom. Try not to paint directly over the seam or the tin will be hard to open after it dries. Let dry, then apply a second coat. Let that dry, too.

4. Hold the tin from the sides and paint the top and bottom. Rest the tin on its side and let dry. Apply a second coat and let that dry, too.

5. Arrange the paper scraps, photos, and clippings on top of the tin. Don't glue them down until you like the layout. Now it's time to glue. Start with the items you want in the background, such as the larger scraps of paper. Apply a drop of white craft glue to the back of each paper piece and spread it around with your finger. Wipe your finger clean, then place the paper on the tin and smooth out any bubbles. Let dry for a few minutes and then add the pictures you want on top, using the same gluing process. Let dry.

6. Use the paint pens to write or doodle on the top and sides of the tin. Let dry.

7. Dip your brush in the varnish and paint a layer on the tin, first holding the top and bottom to varnish the sides (remember not to paint directly over the seam). Let it dry, then hold the sides to varnish the top and bottom. Let dry again, then repeat to give it a second coat.

8. Repeat the above steps to decorate the inside. Let dry and then fill with treasures!

Other Ideas

❀ Make a little photo album inside the tin. Cut out a strip of construction paper 2 inches wide and 10 inches long. Fold it back and forth, like an accordion. Use the paint pens to write or doodle on each "panel" and glue on tiny photos of your friends, or write little poems or notes. Apply white glue to the last flap of the folded strip and press it into the bottom of the tin. Let dry for 15–20 minutes. You can hold your little book closed with a neat-looking paper clip. Then close the tin.

❀ Use a breath-strip container as a mini frame to "hang" on the inside of the tin's lid. Just snip off the front flap of the breath-strip container. Cut out a photo to fit, then glue it inside the lid. Very cool!

❀ Add more glitzy elements to liven up your tin, such as tiny flowers, sequins, and rhinestones. Use white craft glue to apply them to the sides, top, and insides of the tin.

- Prides herself on making handmade cards and gifts for everyone in the family.

- Single-handedly solves daily household crises by being the understanding referee.

- Can organize a family function with just thirty minutes notice.

Whether her family is as small as two or a big as twelve, the FAMILY BONDER is best friends with each member in some certain way, and vice versa. They all dig her because they know she puts them before all else. Is your family the best thing to happen to you since, well, forever? If so, keep the good energy flowing with projects that give new flair to the term "family fun."

Fortune Cookie Frame

Cheer-Me-up Flowers

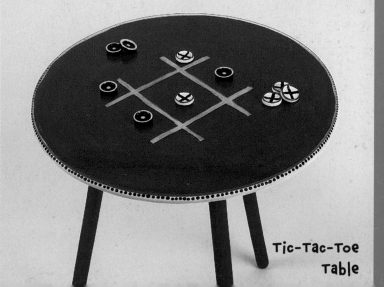

Tic-Tac-Toe Table

Fortune Cookie FRAME

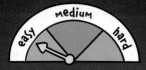

Egg rolls are tasty, but they aren't the main reason you and your family head out to a Chinese dinner. It's all about the fortune cookies. There's never a gloomy message in the bunch—how can anyone **Not** like them? It's such a shame when, after a night of chowing down on shrimp chow mein, those little paper notes get left behind. Here's your next assignment: At the end of the meal, collect and save them so you can show them off on a rad picture frame like the ones shown here.

Stuff You'll Need

- wooden picture frame with a wide border
- fortunes
- little things to add to your frame, like chopsticks, coins, flower pictures, plastic bugs, etc. (optional)
- craft acrylic paints in assorted colors and paintbrush
- Aleene's Original Tacky Glue
- white craft glue and foam brush
- Delta Sparkle Varnish and brush

How to Do It

1. Paint the top and sides of your frame in whatever color you like. Let dry.

2. Lay out the fortunes on the frame so they look nice and balanced. Pick up one fortune at a time and paint the back of it with a thin layer of white craft glue, then press it into place. Smooth out any bubbles with your fingers. Repeat the process to attach the other fortunes. Brush a thin layer of white craft glue over the top of the fortunes to seal them onto the frame. Let dry.

3. Brush a layer of sparkle varnish over the entire surface and let dry. This will add a shimmery effect to your frame. If you don't have sparkle varnish, regular varnish is fine.

4. Use the tacky glue to add other small objects in between the fortunes. Let dry.

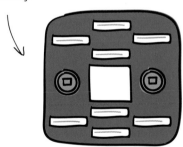

5. Add a photo of your family, and display!

Other Ideas

● Does your family *love* Chinese food? If so, you'll have lots of chances to collect fortunes. Make more frames and group them all together.

● Take a picture the next time you're eating Chinese food with your family, then use the photo in the frame.

Cheer-Me-Up FLOWERS

easy — medium — hard

Everyone needs cheering up once in a while—especially our families. Go into your room for a top-secret mission of making each member a perky paper flower. They're so colorful and happy looking, everyone will love you for the thought!

Stuff You'll Need

- tissue-paper party streamers in assorted colors
- green pipe cleaners
- loose glitter in assorted colors
- white craft glue
- 2 paper plates
- scissors

How to Do It

1. Unroll one of the party streamers and cut off a piece 6 inches long. Cut another piece the same size from a different color. Lay the two strips on top of each other.

2. Place a pipe cleaner along the end of the paper strips. Pinch the bottom edge of the paper around the pipe cleaner. Slowly roll the paper, holding the bottom in place as you turn but letting the top of the paper fan out.

3. When you get to the end of the paper, tightly wrap the pipe cleaner twice around the bottom so the flower won't come undone. You can also secure it with a piece of scotch tape if you like.

4. Pour some white glue onto a paper plate. Sprinkle a small pile of glitter into another paper plate. Gently dip the ends of your flower into the glue—just enough to lightly coat the edges.

Now dip and roll the flower in the glitter. Blow off any excess. Stand the flower upright in a tall container until dry.

Other Ideas

- Make a garland of flowers to hang on your wall. Cut a long piece of string, then tie a knot around the base of each flower in a line along the string. Trim off the extra pipe cleaners.

- Mix and match the flower colors to make a bouquet that will never wilt!

TIC-TAC-TOE Table

There are two awesome things about this project. First, it's always ready to go for a mind-twisting tic-tac-toe championship. Second, it looks very chic just sitting there, minding its own business as a regular room accessory.

Tip You don't really need to use a glass top. Your table will work just as well without it. The glass is there to protect your work (it cleans up easily with glass cleaner) and make the table look nice.

Stuff You'll Need

- lightweight, round table with removable legs and glass top (found at discount department stores)
- 10 small wooden discs, about the size of checkers
- black craft acrylic paint
- craft acrylic paint in four contrasting colors (see "tip")
- thin liner brush
- foam brush
- Delta Sparkle Varnish (or regular varnish) and brush

How to Do It

1. Carefully set the glass top aside. Remove the table legs if possible. Paint the top and legs of the table in a color of your choice. Then paint five of the wooden discs in a color that contrasts with the table. Paint the other five discs in a second, contrasting color. Let dry.

Tip To make your work "pop," use colors that contrast boldly against each other, like red and green, blue and orange, or yellow and purple.

2. Paint the edge of the tabletop with another bright color. Let dry. Decorate with dots or squiggles.

3. Look for a tiny bump in the center of the tabletop—that's where the center square will go. Use the liner brush to paint two lines down and two lines across.

4. Use the liner brush to paint an "X" on five of the wooden disks and an "O" on the other five.

5. Let everything dry, then brush on a layer of sparkle varnish. Let dry overnight.

6. Reassemble the table and carefully place the glass on top. Put the game pieces on the glass. Let the tournament begin! X goes first....

Other Ideas

- Tired of tic-tac-toe? No problem. Paint over the tabletop and do an outline for checkers or backgammon instead.

@ Knows exactly what NOT to wear.

@ Never wears the same outfit more than once in the same month (the horror!).

@ Madly scribbles notes while watching cable fashion shows, then uses her crafty wiles to re-create the looks for herself.

The mall has nothing on the **FLASHY FASHIONISTA**. She yawns at all those adorable outfits in the store windows because, let's face it, she's been wearing them for months already! Style mavens don't wait around for the next hot trend—they come up with their own. Sometimes that means taking a pair of scissors to a frumpy, worn-out tee. And that's a good thing.

Swirly Glitter Jeans

Funky Baby-Doll Shirt

Pant-Leg Purse

Swirly GLITTER JEANS

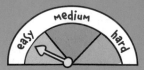

Blue jeans are a fashion must, no doubt about that. One reason is because they are a blank canvas eager to be embellished. Great, bring on the bleach pen! This is the coolest product invented since glitter glue. Watch, learn, and you will understand why.

Stuff You'll Need

@ pair of jeans
@ Clorox Bleach Pen (found in the laundry aisle at the grocery store)
@ fabric glitter spray
@ paper towels

How to Do It

1. Bleach is stinky, so work in a well-ventilated area, like on a table in the backyard. Lay the jeans out, with the front facing up. Pull off the cap from the fine-tip side of the bleach pen and squeeze out the gel in swirly designs on the pockets, belt loops, and at the bottom of the legs. Let it set for 30 minutes if the jeans are thick or 15 minutes if they are really thin.

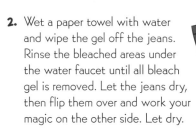

2. Wet a paper towel with water and wipe the gel off the jeans. Rinse the bleached areas under the water faucet until all bleach gel is removed. Let the jeans dry, then flip them over and work your magic on the other side. Let dry.

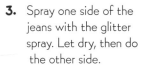

3. Spray one side of the jeans with the glitter spray. Let dry, then do the other side.

Tip

Use a pencil and paper to practice your designs first. There's no need to stick to swirls—the sky's the limit. You might also try some of the doodles from page 136.

Other Ideas

@ Don't stop with your jeans! You can use the bleach pen on pillowcases, tote bags, backpacks, holiday stockings, and more. Ask a parental unit for permission before diving in.

4. Wash and dry your jeans using a normal cycle before wearing them. If the glitter fades after a while, just spray on another layer.

Funky BABY-DOLL SHIRT

Before you toss that pile of old T-shirts, look at them again with a new set of eyes: designer eyes. If you like the print but the shirt's body has seen better days, salvage it by trimming the neckline, arms, and bottom into an updated shape. Add some trim to cover the edges and you'll have one groovy garment.

Stuff You'll Need

@ old T-shirt
@ 2 types of trim (1 yard of each)
@ squeeze-on glitter (optional)
@ sequins in assorted colors (optional)
@ Aleene's OK To Wash-It fabric glue
@ fabric pencil
@ paper
@ measuring tape
@ scissors

How to Do It

1. Take a piece of paper and sketch out some ideas of how to tailor the shirt.

2. Put the shirt on. Using the fabric pencil, make light, small dots to show how much you want to cut from it. For example, if you want it to end 2 inches below your belly button, make a dot there. Think modest when it comes to cutting the neckline and the bottom—you don't want to look all hootchie-mama!

3. Take the shirt off and lay it flat on the table. Using the dots and your sketch as guides, lightly draw lines on the shirt where you want to cut it.

4. Cut along your lines. Make sure you cut through both layers.

Other Ideas

@ Add a tie-dye look by using different colors of spray-on fabric paint. ·

5. Place the measuring tape along the bottom of the shirt. Multiply this number by 2—that's how many inches of trim you'll need to cover both sides. Cut that amount of trim. Now measure the neckline and multiply by 2. Cut that amount of trim, too. Do the same for each armhole.

6. Squeeze a thin line of fabric glue along the bottom of the shirt. Place the trim along the glue and run your fingers over it so it will stick in place. Do not cut off the extra trim—you will wrap it around to the back later. Glue trim onto the neckline and armholes as well. Let dry. Flip the shirt over and glue the extra trim onto the back.

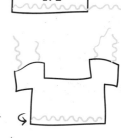

7. Brighten up the shirt by gluing on sequins with squeeze-on glitter paint (put a dot of paint on the shirt, then press the sequin onto it). Let dry. Wash on regular cycle, but turn the shirt inside out.

Pant-Leg PURSE

The first lesson for a crafty diva is to know when to salvage something—like that favorite pair of jeans you outgrew this year. There's no reason to pout, you can keep the memory of those soft and comfy pants. They'll just be in a slightly different form.

Stuff You'll Need

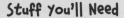

- @ pair of straight-legged jeans
- @ 1 yard of decorative trim
- @ 1 yard of wide trim (to be used as the strap)
- @ extra-strong thread and thick needle
- @ Aleene's OK To Wash-It fabric glue
- @ measuring tape
- @ straight pins
- @ scissors

How to Do It

1. Cut off the bottom part of one leg of the jeans, just above the knee area. Set the rest of the jeans aside.

Tip 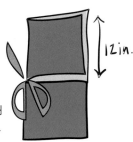 You can use fabric glue for this project, but your purse won't be as strong or last as long as if you sew it.

2. Take the leg portion you just cut off. Lay it on the table. Starting at the top, cut down one side seam for 12 inches. Then cut all the way across the front and up the other side. You've just created the "flap" to close your purse.

12 in.

3. Turn the pant leg inside out. Thread your needle and sew the bottom together, right above the jean's thick hem. (See "How to Sew by Hand," opposite.) Sew a second row in the opposite direction, so your purse will be extra sturdy.

4. Turn the pant leg right side out again. Now you want to make a hem around the sides of the flap. Make a ¼-inch fold around all three edges of the flap and pin in place. Thread your needle and sew the hem in place.

5. Add the strap. Open the flap and pin one end of the strap to the inner side of the bag, about 1 inch down. Pin the other end of the strap to the other side.

6. Thread your needle and sew the ends of the strap to the purse. Don't just sew one line across the strap—sew a square, as shown, so your purse can hold heavy items.

7. Use the fabric glue to attach trim along the edge of the flap or the bottom of the purse.

8. Now that you've got the hang of it, move on to the second leg of your jeans and make another purse, either for yourself or a friend!

Other Ideas

@ Once you get going, cut off other parts of the jeans—like the back pocket or the belt loops—and add them to the outside of your purse.

@ To make your purse really "pop," iron on funky patches.

How to Sew by Hand

1. Cut a piece of thread 24 inches long. Lick the end of the thread to make a sharp point. Hold your needle up to the light and insert the end of the thread through the hole.

2. Pull the thread all through until it's doubled, with the needle in the middle. Tie the two strands of thread together in a double knot.

3. Insert the needle from underneath the fabric and poke it up through to the other side. Pull the needle and thread all the way through until it stops.

4. Skip about a ¼-inch space and poke the needle back down through the fabric, again pulling until it stops.

5. Skip another ¼-inch space. Poke the needle up through the fabric and pull. Congratulations, you've learned the running stitch! If you're sewing a hem, try to work in a straight line along the edge of the fabric.

6. Continue until you reach the end of the fabric. At that point, sew an extra stitch over your last one to secure the fabric. Flip over the fabric and make a double knot on the underside to make sure your hard work doesn't come undone.

Garden Goddess

- Likes to see the fruits of her labors...and to eat them, too.

- Doesn't mind getting a little dirt under her glitter-polished fingernails.

- Loves to stop and smell the roses—every day!

The **GARDEN GODDESS** is a modern-day flower child—she knows the true value of taking a breath of fresh air. She's always the one to get everyone outside, smelling the flowers and rolling around in the grass, and is often seen with a flower in her hair. For those of you who love all things blooming and natural, here are three crafty projects to make your inner garden glow.

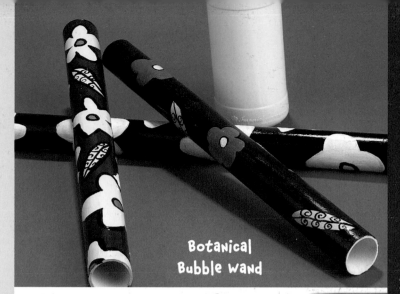

Botanical Bubble Wand

Flower "Empower" Pots

Flower Fairy Headband

Botanical BUBBLE WAND

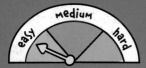

Introducing the magnificent bubble wand, ready to be dipped into a magical potion of suds. Long gone are the days of those chintzy plastic kiddy wands—we've moved on to our own variation, cleverly made from PVC pipe (available at any hardware store).

Stuff You'll Need

- piece of PVC pipe, 12 inches long and ¾ inch in diameter
- craft acrylic paints in assorted colors and paintbrush
- black permanent marker
- medium-grit sandpaper
- water-based varnish and brush

How to Do It

1. Sand the ends of the PVC pipe until they're smooth. Wipe off any dust.

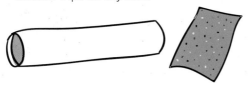

2. Paint the entire outer surface of the pipe with a color of your choice. Let dry.

3. Decorate your bubble-blower-to-be with painted designs. Check out Doodling 101 on page 136, use the Clip Art Treasure Chest on page 138, or try your own designs. Let dry.

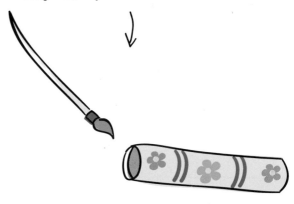

4. Carefully outline your designs with the marker. (Read "How to Outline," at right.) Let dry.

5. Gently rub your finger over your work to make sure it's dry. Brush on a layer of varnish to seal your A-plus paint job.

6. Mix up the magical bubble potion (see recipe below). Or, if you're anxious to make bubbles and want a shortcut, pick up a bottle of pre-mixed bubble solution from the store. Dip your blower into the solution, pull it out, and blow through the other end. You'll love the mega-sized bubbles it makes! Try blowing short and fast to make different shapes and sizes.

How to Outline

Outlining can be stressful, especially when using a permanent marker. Relax, it's easier than it seems. The trick is to keep your hand steady. Hold your pen like you normally do, but before you start, anchor your pinky finger tightly against the surface to keep your hand still. Carefully and slowly trace the outside of each design or letter. This will make your shapes and words look very bold. It's okay if you mess up—any little squiggles will make your work look handmade and unique. If you happen to make a *big* mistake, don't freak out. Just let the ink dry, then paint over it with the base color to cover it. Now that wasn't so bad, was it?

Magical Bubble Potion

- 1 cup liquid dish detergent
- 2 cups warm water
- ½ teaspoon sugar
- 1 teaspoon glycerin
- container with lid

Mix all of the ingredients together in a bowl, then pour into a container with a lid for future use. Don't forget to label it in bold letters that say "Magical Bubble Potion"—you don't want your brother thinking it's mouthwash, do you? By the way, glycerin is used to make soap and can be found at the craft store.

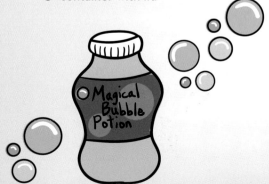

Flower "EMPOWER" POTS

Just like us, plants and flowers need vitamins, water, food, sunshine, and—most importantly—an inspiring environment in which to grow. That magical extra touch can be added to your garden, bedroom, patio, or school desk with one of these uplifting planter's pots. Use a short poem or just random words that make you smile.

How to Do It

1. Paint the outside of the pots in whatever color you like. Apply two to three coats, and be patient—let each layer dry before applying the next. If you don't, the paint will smudge and you will have to paint them all over again.

2. Before diving into the painted letters, practice them on a piece of paper. Use the letters on page 137 as a guide. Once you have the hang of it, take a deep breath and start painting the words on the pots. Make sure to leave a lot of space between letters so you'll have room to outline them later. Let dry.

Stuff You'll Need

- 4-inch terra-cotta pots and saucers
- craft acrylic paints in assorted colors and paintbrush
- fine-point permanent black marker
- water-based varnish and brush

3. Outline your words with the black marker (see "How to Outline" on page 67). Let dry for at least 30 minutes.

4. Gently rub your finger over the painted surface to make sure it's completely dry. Using the foam brush, cover the entire surface of the pot with a layer of varnish.

Other Ideas

- Make a decoupage pot. Use white craft glue to apply cutout pictures or phrases to the pot. Keep adding them until the entire surface is covered. Let dry, then seal it by brushing on a layer of water-based varnish.

- Instead of words, paint abstract shapes or flowers.

Flower Fairy HEADBAND

When was the last time you put flowers in your hair? If it's been a while, here's a snap-tastic way to look absolutely darling: this floral fantasy of a headband. Or you could call it a flowered tiara. Whatever. All it takes is a batch of colorful silk flowers and green pipe cleaners to liven up an otherwise ho-hum hairpiece.

Stuff You'll Need

- wide headband with a smooth surface
- 8–10 green pipe cleaners
- silk flowers
- Aleene's Original Tacky Glue
- scissors

How to Do It

1. Take one of the pipe cleaners and, starting at one end of the headband, wrap it tightly around the surface to cover it. Keep going with more pipe cleaners until the entire headband is covered. It should look green and fuzzy.

2. Pull the flowers and leaves off of their stems and put them in separate piles. Snip the silk leaves apart so they look like individual leaves.

3. Add a small drop of tacky glue to the bottom side of one leaf and place it, pointy side out, on top of the headband. Hold in place for a minute. Add a few more leaves on both sides until they look balanced.

4. Take one flower at a time and add a dab of glue to its bottom. Quickly place the flower on the top of the headband and hold it place for a few seconds. Keep adding flowers along the top of the headband until you like how it looks. Try alternating colors and flower styles for an ultra garden-y look.

Other Ideas

- Feeling wild? Wrap two green pipe cleaners around the top of the headband and bend them in swirls for cute bug antennae. Or wrap a strand of shiny-star garland (found at craft stores) around it for a disco garden look (see picture on page 65).

Garden Goddess   69

- ⚙ wears out her fluffy slippers before her tennis shoes.

- ⚙ Rearranges her bedroom at the beginning of each season.

- ⚙ Loves nothing better than a rainy day, a pile of DVDs, and a full box of microwave popcorn.

When people call the HAPPY HOMEBODY "home girl," they aren't kidding. She really likes to hang out on the couch, with the remote and the latest issue of TV Guide nearby. For the sake of HGTV already, take a break from the couch potato lifestyle! Move that booty over to the art table and get cracking on these fabulous room accessories. When you are done, you will be allowed to return to the couch.

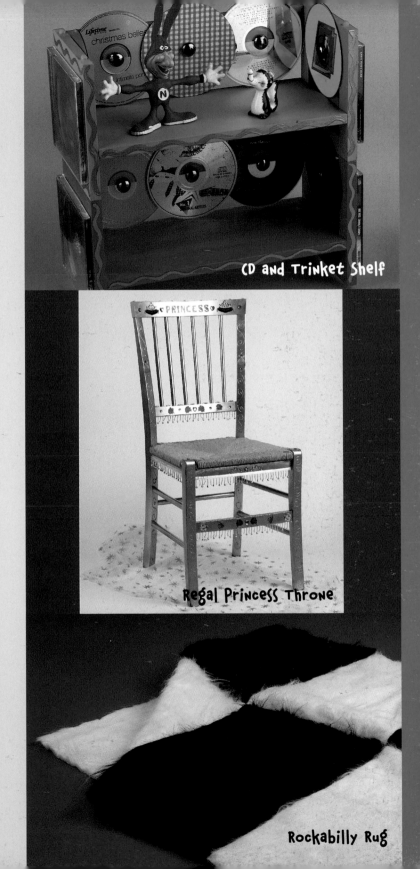

CD and Trinket Shelf

Regal Princess Throne

Rockabilly Rug

CD and TRINKET SHELF

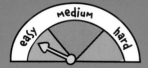

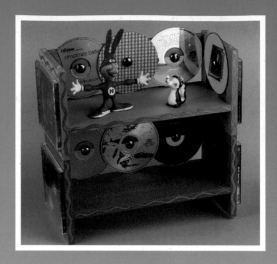

Are you tired of walking back and forth between your stereo or computer and your CD rack? You'd be considered borderline lazy if it weren't for your being so crafty. Streamline your routine by creating a little CD-and-trinket shelf for your desk or nightstand. Choose your favorite discs and set them in this little unit. You can also use the top shelf for goofy toys or small pictures.

Stuff You'll Need

- 2 stackable CD shelves, wooden or plastic
- 10 unwanted, unusable, or free CDs
- 4 empty CD jewel cases
- 10 colored glass pebbles (from the pet store or the floral department at the craft store)
- 2 colors of craft acrylic paint and paintbrush
- E6000 glue
- medium-grit sandpaper
- water-based varnish and brush

How to Do It

1. Lightly sand the stackable shelves. This will help the paint "grip" the surface. Wipe off any dust.

2. Paint one shelf in one color, the other in another color. Let dry. Paint wavy lines or dots along the edges and let that dry, too. Brush on a coat of varnish. Let dry.

3. Take five of the CDs and put a dab of E6000 glue on the back of each. Set three of them in a row along the inside back of one shelf, as shown. Use two more for the inside ends. To decorate the outside, glue a jewel case on each end. Repeat all of this for the second shelf.

4. Put a dab of glue on the back of each glass pebble and set one in the center of each CD. You will have to hold them in place for a few minutes until they set. Let dry overnight.

5. Stack the shelves, fill with your favorite CDs and trinkets, and use!

Tip The jewel cases on the outside are perfect spots to keep your all-time favorite CDs. They'll be super easy to get to, and they're in a top-secret spot.

Regal Princess THRONE

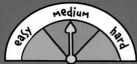

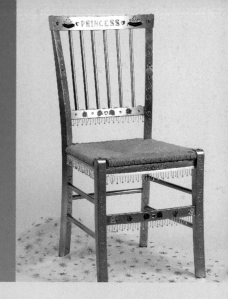

Your bedroom, as small or large as it may be, is your own private castle. Behind that door, you rule the land as you see fit. No princess should be without her royal throne. It's a regal place to sit and ponder life's great questions like, "I wonder what's on the lunch menu tomorrow?" or "Did Mom wash my gym shorts last night?"

Stuff You'll Need

- old wooden chair (ask before painting!)
- silver craft acrylic paint
- pink craft acrylic paint
- silver 3-D squeeze paint
- 1 or 2 packages of pink and/or clear gems
- 2 packages of fringe
- letter and flower stickers
- Aleene's Original Tacky Glue
- medium-grade sandpaper
- paintbrush
- Delta Sparkle Varnish and brush

How to Do It

1. Lightly sand the chair so the paint will grip it. Wipe off any dust. Then paint the entire chair silver and the seat area pink. (It doesn't matter if the seat is wood or straw, either can be painted.) Add at least three layers of paint, letting each one dry in between.

2. Brush on two layers of varnish, letting each one dry in between.

3. Apply the letter stickers to spell out "princess" or your name along the top of the chair. Use the tacky glue to put gems and stickers on both ends. Add more stickers and rhinestones to decorate the front of the chair.

4. Run a line of tacky glue along the edge of the fringe and press it along the bottom of the chair's back. Glue more fringe under the chair's seat, or wherever you want. Let dry.

5. Lay the chair on its back, then add swirls to the front with the 3-D squeeze paint. Let dry.

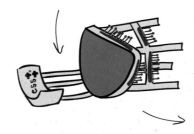

Other Ideas

- Add a tie-on pillow cushion to make your throne even cushier.

ROCKABILLY Rug

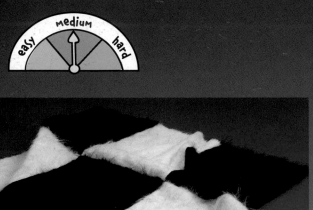

If you're a fan of hanging out at home, you know the value of a decent fake fur rug. Imagine coming home after a long day at school, tossing your books on the bed, and plopping down on this luxurious black and white rug. You won't just look like one of those happy homeowners on "Trading Spaces"—you'll be one!

Stuff You'll Need

- 1 yard of fake black fur (found at the fabric store)
- 1 yard of fake white fur
- extra-strong thread and thick needle (or sewing machine)
- straight pins
- scissors

How to Do It

1. Take the white fur and fold it in half so the fur is on the inside. Cut along the fold. Now take one of those pieces, fold it in half again (fur inside) and cut up that fold. Do the same for the other piece you cut.

2. Repeat step 1 for the black fur. You should end up with eight rectangles of fur (four white and four black). Set aside one rectangle of each color—you don't need them.

3. Take one piece of white fur and one of black. Put them together with the fur facing in and the fur strands going down. Pin them together along the top edge. Sew along the pins, using the running stitch (see "How to Sew by Hand" on page 63). Remove the pins.

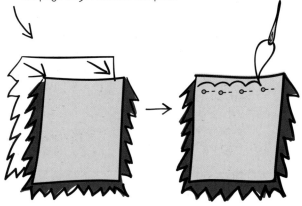

4. Repeat step 3 with two more pieces of white and black fur. Then repeat again with the last two pieces. You should end up with three double pieces, each half white and half black.

5. Arrange the three pieces so they look like the picture. One row should be black, white, black; the other row should be white, black, white. They're opposites, get it?

6. Now for the last step: assembling the pieces. You're going to sew these larger pieces together just as you did the smaller pieces in step 3. Put the first two pieces together, fur side in, and pin along the long edge. Sew them together, then remove the pins.

7. Now put the third piece over the middle piece, fur side in. Pin, and sew (make sure you're sewing the correct edge, so when you unfold your rug it will lie right). Remove the pins, unfold, and enjoy your stylin' new rug.

Words of Wisdom

Be inspired! Walk with your eyes open and see the amazing world around you. Do what you can to make your life amazing. Don't think mistakes won't happen. But don't punish yourself for what you did wrong. Instead, think about the mistake and learn from it.

—Vanessa Brady, 25, purse designer and seamstress (www.gerberadesigns.com)

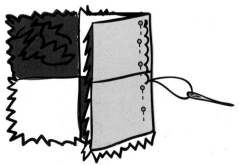

Other Ideas

- Fake fur comes in all kinds of colors—pick ones that match your bedroom.

- Make a pillow with the two leftover pieces of fur.

- ★ Likes to watch romantic comedies with a box of tissues, chocolate, and a bag of gourmet popcorn.

- ★ Always wants—let's face it, expects—the movie-star treatment.

- ★ Knows how to make a grand entrance, pen in hand for any autograph seekers.

The **HOLLYWOOD DIVA** knows how to take command of an audience because show biz is her middle name. Like any true celeb, she spends hours pondering her best side, and has been spotted more than once wearing sunglasses at night. But what's a Hollywood diva without some savvy accessories to match? Here are three projects to amp up your already high-wattage status quo. It's all about star power, baby.

Sassy Stationery

Celebrity Bedroom Lights

Hollywood Robe

Sassy STATIONERY

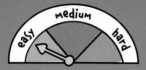

Store-bought stationery is okay for normal people, but divas need flash—even when it comes to the paper they scribble on. So what's a girl to do? Take the matter into your own creative little hands, that's what. When you're done, you'll have a fab set of one-of-a-kind stationery to send to friends, family, and of course—talent agents.

Stuff You'll Need

★ piece of white, unlined paper
★ markers and pens in assorted sizes
★ rubber cement or glue stick
★ scissors

How to Do It

1. Ask a parent or older sibling to take you to the local copy shop. Make a black-and-white photocopy of the face design you want to use from the Clip Art Treasure Chest on page 139. This will be the focal point of your stationery.

2. Most copy shops have a table stocked with scissors, tape, rubber cement, and other supplies, so you can assemble your stationery right there. Cut out the copy of your face design and brush a thin layer of rubber cement on the back. Press it onto a corner of your blank white paper.

3. Use the markers to write your name in neat letters under the face and add all kinds of fun doodles (check out pages 136–137 for ideas). You've now created your "master template."

4. Now it's time to make your actual stationery. Using a black-and-white copy machine, place your template on the glass. Punch in the number of copies you want. If you want your stationery on colored paper, ask an attendant to help you. That's what they're there for!

Other Ideas

★ Neatly line up all of your sheets and paint a thick layer of rubber cement along the top to create a notepad.

★ Create a set of cards by decorating only the bottom half of your template. After you photocopy the template, fold each paper in half to make a card.

Celebrity BEDROOM LIGHTS

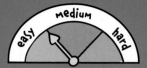

You've put a lot of sweat and tears into those acting, dancing, and singing classes, hoping some day it will all pay off. Girl, it will. Today you may be playing an angel in the school holiday play, but years from now you'll have top billing on Broadway. In the meantime, these lights will add some inspiration to your hopes and dreams.

Stuff You'll Need

* ★ set of decorative indoor star-shaped lights (other shapes are fine, too)
* ★ gold or silver 3-D squeeze paint
* ★ pencil and paper
* ★ Delta Sparkle Varnish and brush

How to Do It

1. Count how many lights come in the set (usually it's 10 or 12). Take the lights out of the box and lay them right side up on a table.

2. The number of lights is also the number of letters you can use (you'll be putting one letter on each light). Jot down short phrases with the pencil and paper that will fit. Think cool. Think movie star cool. Think red runway carpet cool. If you're too shy to be *that* cool, use your name. If your name is too long, use a nickname. If you are using short words, leave one blank light in between each word.

3. With a steady hand, use the squeeze paint to write one letter in the center of each light. Let dry for several hours.

4. Brush on a layer of sparkle varnish for a shimmery look. Let dry and then hang up and plug in. Don't worry about the paint getting damaged from the light's heat. The mini bulbs are such low wattage that your wonderful work won't be affected.

Other Ideas

* ★ Paint your lights with crazy colors first. Let dry and then add the letters.

Tip

Can't think of what to write? Here are a few ideas to get the juices flowing:

superstar	smile big
crafty diva	whatever!
goddess	you go girl
movie star	kiss kiss
Hollywood	cutie pie

Hollywood ROBE

After a long night of glamour and fun, a bath and a fluffy pillow sound pretty good. A diva does need her eight hours of beauty sleep, after all. But that doesn't mean you have to resort to a frumpy ensemble for bedtime. Try this recipe for jazzing up your robe. Even if it's two in the morning and the rest of the family is snoring in bed, you'll look gorgeous pouring that glass of warm milk.

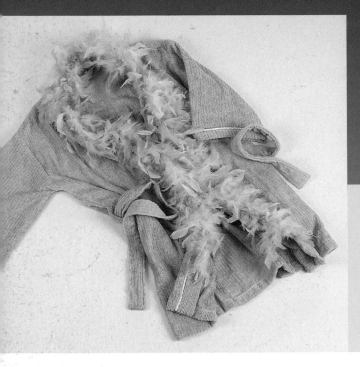

Stuff You'll Need

★ bathrobe
★ boa, fluffy or feathered (can be found at the craft or fabric store)
★ needle and thread
★ safety pin
★ scissors

How to Do It

1. Cut a piece of thread 14 inches long. Thread it through the needle. Pull the thread through until the needle is in the middle, then tie the ends in a quadruple knot. Cut off the extra thread, leaving a 2-inch tail after the knot.

2. Now you are going to "tack" the boa to the robe. It's much easier than it sounds! Fold the boa in half to find the middle. Keep your finger on that spot and place it at the top and center of the robe's collar (use the label on the robe as a guide). Pin the boa in place.

3. Starting from underneath the collar, poke the needle up through the robe, very close to where you've pinned the boa. Pull the needle and thread toward you until it stops. Wrap the thread over the boa, then poke the needle back down through the fabric to the back. Repeat. Tie the two ends in a knot and cut off the extra thread.

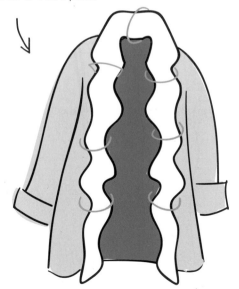

4. Repeat the process every 6 inches down both sides of the front of the robe. When you're done, be sure to store the needle in a safe place.

Tip

Eventually, you will have to wash your bathrobe. To do this you first need to remove the boa or it will be ruined. Just take the scissors and snip the thread wherever the boa is tacked on. Sew the boa back on when the robe is clean. Yup, it takes a bit of effort, but beauty is pain. If you *never* want to wash your robe, you can use fabric glue to attach the boa, but it can get a bit messy.

Other Ideas

★ Buy another boa and use it to trim an eye mask, headband, or nightgown.

★ If you're really flashy, cut a sweatshirt up the front and use that instead of the bathrobe.

★ Use Aleene's Original Tacky Glue to add pieces of boa to your slippers or a pair of flip-flops.

5. Model your new ensemble and blow a kiss to yourself in the mirror for completing such a great-looking project!

- Must have all things that shimmer, dangle, or flash.

- Will put a hole in almost anything to create a necklace or pair of earrings.

- Wears charm bracelets and toe rings to gym class.

Picture Bracelet

The **JEWELRY HOUND** is the queen bee of artsy accessories. She can turn blah into bling-bling with just one flash of a ring or bracelet. Now that's talent. You know you have it if you can't step one foot into the lunchroom without someone asking, "Ooooo, where did you get that?" After making the divine designs in this section, you can simply answer, "Oh, it's nothing, just a little something I put together."

Chunky Hair Clips

Roundabout Rings

Picture BRACELET

Don't even think about leaving home without at least one piece of arm candy—that means a bracelet. Rather than going the usual beaded route like every other Jenny on the block, make an individual statement by creating a one-of-a-kind masterpiece.

Stuff You'll Need

- 6 small pictures from magazines, gift wrap, photos, stationery, or rubber-stamped designs
- 6 flat washers, each ¾ inch in diameter
- 6 silver bola tie slides (found at the craft store)
- 7 jump rings
- lobster clasp
- Aleene's Original Tacky Glue
- E6000 glue
- tracing paper and pencil
- scissors

How to Do It

1. Lay a washer on the tracing paper and outline its shape with the pencil. Cut out the shape. This is your picture template.

2. Lay the template on top of each picture to make sure the image will fit. Trace around the template onto each picture and cut out the pictures.

3. Put a dot of tacky glue on one side of a washer and rub it from end to end. Wipe your fingers clean, then press a picture firmly onto the glue. Repeat for the other washers/pictures. Let dry.

4. Put a dab of E6000 glue on the back of a bola tie slide. Place it on the back of one of the washers so the slide goes straight across (make sure your picture faces the right way). Set facedown to dry. Repeat for the other washers. Let dry for several hours.

5. Open a jump ring and attach it to one end of a bola tie slide, then use your fingers to bend it shut. Attach a second jump ring to the other end of the tie slide. Before you squeeze the jump ring shut, attach it to another tie slide, linking the pieces of your bracelet together. Continue until all six washers are connected.

6. When you run out of washers, attach the last jump ring to the end, slide on the lobster clasp, and squeeze the jump ring shut.

Other Ideas

- Make a ring by gluing a decorated washer onto a ring blank, as in the photo. Ring blanks are available at craft stores.

Chunky HAIR CLIPS

There are times when you should let your locks flow freely. And then there are times when all you want to do is wear a ski cap. Hold on, there's no need to get all drastic about it! Just wear one of these cute clay barrettes and no one will notice the hair underneath. That's what being crafty is all about.

Stuff You'll Need

- metal hair clip, 3 inches long
- polymer clay in assorted colors
- E6000 glue
- plastic knife
- craft acrylic paints and paintbrush, rhinestones, and/or fine glitter (all optional)
- cookie sheet
- water-based varnish and brush

How to Do It

1. Pinch off a piece of clay, about the size of a silver dollar. Roll it into a ball. Now roll the ball on a clean, flat surface to form a small log the same size as the hair clip.

2. Place the log on the hair clip and carefully press it so it covers the entire surface, but don't let the clay go over the sides.

3. Pinch off another piece of clay in a different color and roll it into a strand, like a piece of thin spaghetti. Place one end on the clip and swirl it into a fun design, or create letters. Cut off the extra clay with the plastic knife.

4. Place your clay-covered hair clip on a cookie sheet and bake it in the oven according to the clay package's directions.

5. When the time is up, ask an adult to help you remove the sheet from the oven. Leave it alone until it is cool to the touch (about 20 minutes). Carefully remove the clay from the clip. Add a line of E6000 glue to the top of the clip and set the clay design back on top. Press it firmly (but gently) in place and let dry several hours.

6. Add painted designs, rhinestones, or glitter, or leave it as is. Brush on a coat of varnish, then leave to dry overnight.

Other Ideas

- Use air-dry clay in place of the oven-bake kind. It won't last as long, but it will have the same look.

Hey! Always ask an adult to help you when using the oven or stove. Have pot holders close by and make sure you follow the manufacturer's directions on the package closely.

Roundabout RINGS

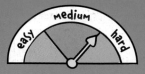

You have ten fingers and ten toes—that's a lot of area to cover. After trying out this ring recipe, you'll be ready to dress up your digits as well as those of your sister or best friend. Heads up, this one looks harder than it is. Take a deep breath, focus on the directions, and go for it.

Stuff You'll Need

- roll of 20-gauge silver wire
- roll of 24-gauge silver wire
- crystal or glass bi-cone (diamond shaped) beads, 14 mm in size
- needle-nose pliers

How to Do It

1. Use the cutting tool on your needle-nose pliers to cut a 12-inch-long strand of the 20-gauge wire. Wrap the strand around whichever finger you want the ring to fit. Wrap it two times for a thin ring or three times for a thick ring. Cut off the extra wire.

2. Cut a piece of the 24-gauge wire into a 12-inch strand. Using the pliers, make a small "hook" at one end. Hook it onto the ring a little bit off center. Wrap the wire snugly around the ring three times, then use the pliers to squeeze the three loops you made tightly around the ring. The rest of the wire should be pointing up.

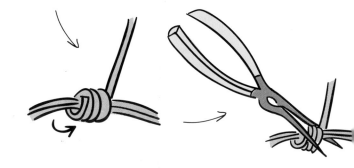

Personalize rings for yourself, friends, and family members by using colors that match your zodiac birthstone. Hello cool birthday presents! Just find the color that goes with your or your friend's zodiac sign, and bead away.

If your birthday is...	your sign is...	and your zodiac birthstone is...
Dec. 22–Jan. 20	Capricorn	ruby (red)
Jan. 21–Feb. 18	Aquarius	garnet (dark red)
Feb. 19–Mar. 20	Pisces	amethyst (purple)
Mar. 21–Apr. 19	Aries	bloodstone (green and red)
Apr. 20–May 20	Taurus	sapphire (blue)
May 21–June 21	Gemini	agate (multicolor)
June 22–July 22	Cancer	emerald (deep green)
July 23–Aug. 22	Leo	onyx (black)
Aug. 23–Sept. 22	Virgo	carnelian (light red)
Sept. 23–Oct. 23	Libra	peridot (light green)
Oct. 24–Nov. 22	Scorpio	beryl (yellow)
Nov. 23–Dec. 21	Sagittarius	pink topaz (pink)

Words of Wisdom

Don't get caught up in taking other people's advice. People will want to help you improve, but if you get too bogged down with trying to please everyone, it will stop being fun. And that's the best part of arts and crafts—it's FUN!

—Audrey Tate, 25, painter, illustrator, and graphic designer (www.audreyart.com)

3. With the wire still pointing up, slide on the first bead. Then wrap the wire around the ring one time. End with the wire pointing up, as it was before. Now slide on the next bead. Wrap the wire around the ring again, ending with the wire pointing up. Continue this process, adding as many beads as you want. Three to five is a good number, but add more if you're feeling flashy.

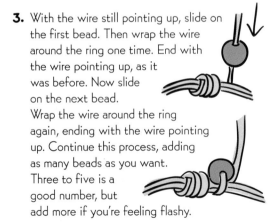

4. When you're done, wrap the rest of the wire around the ring tightly three times, then use the pliers to squeeze the loops in place. Cut off any extra wire.

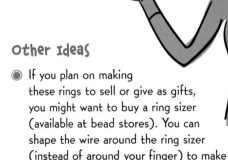

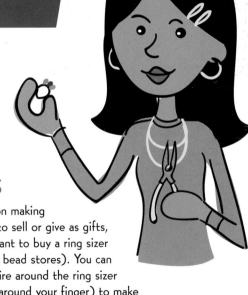

Other Ideas

- If you plan on making these rings to sell or give as gifts, you might want to buy a ring sizer (available at bead stores). You can shape the wire around the ring sizer (instead of around your finger) to make perfect circles.

- Use different colors of wire, or use letter beads instead of plain beads.

- These make great gifts for a party loot bag!

- Have a ring-making party at your house. You can all make rings and then trade them.

- Use the same process to make a beaded bracelet.

Neat Freak

- Puts everything in alphabetical order, even the stuff in her backpack.

- Keeps a bottle of antibacterial hand soap close by at all times.

- Gives her bedroom the "white glove" test at least once a week.

Secret Garden Bulletin Board

Bejeweled Bath Set

The NEAT FREAK isn't a weirdo, she's just more organized than the average person. While the rest of us tend to kick off our shoes and toss our stinky clothes across the room, she takes an extra few minutes to put everything back in place. Okay, you neat types are a little obsessive, but we love you anyway. Just because you're queens of clean doesn't mean you can't be fun, too. To prove it, here are three projects to keep you organized in style!

Lunch-Box Collage Purse

Secret Garden BULLETIN BOARD

Little notes, tickets, and other paper knickknacks are always the first things to get lost when you empty your pockets. The best way to prevent this is to set up a small bulletin board to hold all the goods. While you're at it, you may as well make it a fresh and flowery one. Fun Foam flowers and supplies can be found in the craft store.

Stuff You'll Need

- ⊗ bulletin board with wood frame, 11 x 16 inches
- ⊗ bag of Fun Foam flowers
- ⊗ light-blue craft acrylic paint and foam paintbrush
- ⊗ Fun Foam glue or white craft glue
- ⊗ craft acrylic paint in assorted colors (optional)
- ⊗ liner brush (optional)

How to Do It

1. Using the foam brush, paint the cork area of the bulletin board with two layers of light-blue paint. Let dry between coats.

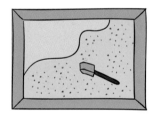

2. Open the bag of Fun Foam flowers. Along with the flowers, there will also be small circles. Sort everything in piles according to size.

3. Arrange the largest sized flowers around the border of the board, leaving spaces in between. Put a generous amount of Fun Foam glue on the back of each flower and press in place. (If you don't have Fun Foam glue, white craft glue will work, too.)

4. One by one, glue the medium flowers in a random pattern around the border, covering the open spaces (it's okay if the flowers touch or overlap). Now glue on the smallest flowers here and there. Glue circles onto the centers of the flowers in the front.

5. If you want more color and design, use the liner brush to paint squiggles or dots on the flowers, as in the photo. Let dry.

Other Ideas

- ⊗ Use this same idea to cover picture frames or mirrors.

Bejeweled BATH SET

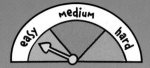

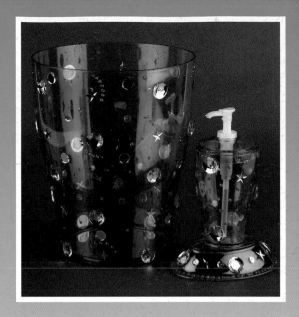

Being clean and tidy has never been so festive! If you don't already have a plastic bathroom accessory set, pick one up at any discount department store. They're cheap, colorful, and a snap to liven up.

How to Do It

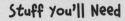

1. Squirt some of the tacky glue onto the paper plate. Gather a handful of the larger gems. Dip the handle of the paintbrush into the glue. Pick up one gem, turn it over, and dab a drop of glue on the back. Press it in place on the wastebasket. Hold it for a few seconds until it stays. Add a few more large gems around the rest of the wastebasket. Do the same for the soap dish and lotion pump.

2. Use the same process to glue on some smaller sized gems. Then add the stars and the mini mirrors. Make sure to keep the amount of each item balanced all over. Let dry.

Stuff You'll Need

- solid-colored plastic bathroom set (waste-basket, soap dish, and lotion pump)
- large bag of silver gems in assorted sizes
- small bag of star-shaped silver sequins
- small bag of mini mirrors
- 3-D squeeze paint in the same color as your bathroom set
- Aleene's Original Tacky Glue
- paintbrush
- paper plate

3. With the squeeze paint, add arcs of small dots by lightly squeezing the paint and quickly dabbing the plastic surface. Put the dots in between the gems, stars, and mini mirrors. Let dry.

Other Ideas

- If your bathroom set comes with more items, like a cup and toothbrush holder, buy more gems to decorate those, too.

- Give your set a rainbow look by using different colored gems, sequins, and stars.

Lunch-Box COLLAGE PURSE

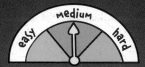

Those of us who are addicted to keeping things organized AND high-fashion handbags always have the same fear: having a sister or pal show up at the mall with the same model. The horror! Here is a way to look like the queen of individuality while still keeping all your personal goods in order. Simply take a blank tin lunch box and cover it in whatever you like: comic books, fashion magazine pictures, or wrapping paper. Anyone else would fill it with a bologna sandwich and chips, but a neat freak like you appreciates its value as a stylish and ultra-organized tote.

Stuff You'll Need

- tin lunch box (found at the craft store)
- comic book, fashion magazine, or assortment of wrapping paper
- craft acrylic paint to accent the edges (any color)
- handful of sequins
- white craft glue and foam brush
- scissors
- Delta Sparkle Varnish and brush

How to Do It

1. Cut out pictures from the comic book or magazine, or rip up pieces of wrapping paper, some large and some small. Hold them up to the lunch box and see how you want to arrange them. Think about covering the top, front, back, and sides.

2. Brush a layer of white glue onto the lunch box, then begin applying the pictures. Use the biggest pictures first, then use smaller pictures to fill any empty spaces. This type of art form is called "collage," and it looks good when pictures are pasted crooked or overlapping. Be sure to smooth down each picture with your fingers to get rid of any bumps or wrinkles underneath. Continue until the entire box is covered. Let dry.

3. Brush a coat of white glue over the entire box. Let dry until glue is clear.

4. Put a dab of paint on your fingertip and carefully run it across all the edges of the box to give it a nice trim. You don't have to do this, but it will make your box look "finished."

5. Use the foam brush to apply a coat of sparkle varnish. (If you don't have sparkle varnish on hand, regular varnish is fine, too.) Let dry.

6. Apply a drop of glue to the back of a sequin and press it in place anywhere on the box. Add more sequins in the same random manner. Let dry, then fill it with all your favorite stuff!

Tip

If you put a large piece of paper on the side of the lunch box and some of it hangs over the rounded edge, it can be tricky to trim off the extra. Here's an easy way to do it: Open your scissors and press one tip under the lip of the upper edge. Move the scissors along the lip to neatly trim off the extra paper.

Other Ideas

- This box is so swell looking that you may want to use it as a real lunch box, an art supply box, or a school supply box for your desk.

- Instead of buying a new lunch box, visit your local thrift store for one that you can revamp.

- ❉ Keeps the numbers of her top fifty friends on speed dial.

- ❉ Is always the first one on the dance floor—sometimes before the music even starts.

- ❉ Dreams of decorating her room with a karaoke machine, disco ball, and strobe light.

When it's time to get the party started, the PARTY PRIESTESS is the one to call. She always comes up with the best ideas and the thriftiest ways to pull them off. That's because she spends half of her time planning parties, and the other half going to them (well, in between school and chores and violin class, that is). If you're a maker and shaker of glam gatherings, you'll love crafting these nifty tricks for your next big bash.

Glow-in-the-Dark Baubles

Gnarly Note Cards

Power Poppers

Glow-in-the-Dark BAUBLES

easy medium hard

It's so hard being the life of the party—everyone always looking to you for tips on fashion, decorating, and accessories. Life is rough. Here's a bright idea to wow your fans: glow-in-the-dark bracelets. Make them wild and crazy or plain and simple. Whip up a batch, keep them under a lamp, and then stack them on your wrists for school dances, trick-or-treating, or heck, even your Aunt Sally's midnight barbecue.

Stuff You'll Need

* glow-in-the-dark polymer clay in assorted colors
* package of Stretch Magic elastic cording, cut into 9-inch strands
* chopstick or bamboo skewer
* cookie sheet

How to Do It

1. Pinch off small pieces of clay and roll them into balls about the size of large marbles. You should be able to make 30–40 balls. Set the balls on a cookie sheet.

2. Get a different color clay and pinch off more pieces. Take one piece and roll it on a flat surface into the shape of a very skinny spaghetti noodle.

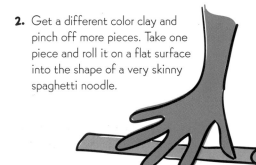

3. Place the clay noodle on one of the balls and lightly wrap it around once or twice. Pinch off the extra and set aside. Pick this ball up and roll it very lightly between your hands, just enough so the noodle blends slightly into the ball. You can also pinch off small dots and press them into the balls. Decorate all the balls with noodles, dots, or other shapes you come up with. Keep them all on the cookie sheet.

4. It's time to poke holes to make the balls into beads. Pick up one ball at a time and gently push the skewer or chopstick all the way through it. Slide it out. Gently press the ball back into shape if needed. Do this for the rest of the clay balls.

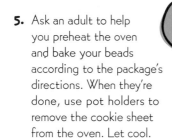

Hey!

Never try to work the oven yourself unless you have specific permission from an adult.

5. Ask an adult to help you preheat the oven and bake your beads according to the package's directions. When they're done, use pot holders to remove the cookie sheet from the oven. Let cool.

6. Take one strand of the elastic cording and string the beads onto it, alternating the colors. For small wrists use six or seven beads, for larger wrists use eight or nine. When you're done, tie the two ends of the cord into a strong double knot and cut off any extra.

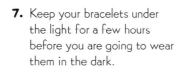

7. Keep your bracelets under the light for a few hours before you are going to wear them in the dark.

Other Ideas

❈ These bracelets are a bit on the Wilma Flintstone side. If you want them to be daintier, just make your beads smaller.

❈ Make a choker necklace or anklet by cutting a longer piece of elastic strand and stringing on more beads.

❈ Make a whole gob of these beads, string them together, and hang them around your room for a groovy nighttime glow.

Gnarly NOTE CARDS

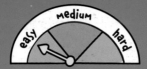

Social gals like you love to write letters. Especially on decked-out note cards that are sassier than your grandma at Friday night bingo. But here's a secret: The fancy set you see here began as a package of blank note cards found in a store clearance bin. For shame! They've come quite a long way, wouldn't you say?

Stuff You'll Need

- ❀ note cards (best if they have a bright image on the front and are blank inside)
- ❀ metallic and glittered shoe stickers (or any other stickers)
- ❀ colored card stock
- ❀ piece of craft foam or thick cardboard
- ❀ glue stick
- ❀ scissors (scrap-booking scissors with curvy edges are best!)

How to Do It

1. Put a sticker on the card stock and cut a square shape around the sticker. If you're using scrap-booking scissors, they will automatically cut a decorative edge for you. If you're using regular scissors, cut the edge of your square into a wavy design. Add other stickers or drawings to decorate the square.

2. Cut a piece of foam board the size of a postage stamp. Glue it to the back of your square.

3. Rub the glue stick on the other side of the foam board and press the whole thing onto the front of the card.

4. Take a sticker and put it in the corner of an envelope to go with the note card.

5. Decorate the rest of your note cards and envelopes in the same way.

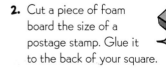

Tip You can also use thick cardboard instead of the foam board. Look around your kitchen or basement for old cardboard boxes that might be thick enough. Be sure to ask before cutting them up.

Other Ideas

- ❀ To use these as party invites, write the details inside with a matching colored pen.
- ❀ Make a set, wrap them up, and give them as a gift!

Power POPPERS

Next time you're working on party favors, bring in the spirit of jolly old England. These little guys have been around since the 1800s! But enough with the history lesson—here's why they're so cool: Inside you hide all kinds of mini treats, like rings, confetti, and candies. One person pulls one end and another person pulls the other end until it "pops" open and all the goodies spray out.

Stuff You'll Need

- ❀ empty paper towel roll (1 per popper)
- ❀ small items to put inside (confetti, plastic jewelry, stickers)
- ❀ scissors
- ❀ scotch tape
- ❀ straight pin
- ❀ piece of wrapping paper, 12 x 12 inches (1 per popper)
- ❀ strands of ribbon, each 6 inches long (2 strands per popper)

How to Do It

1. Cut the paper towel roll in half. Then cut one of the pieces in half again. You should end up with three pieces, one long and two short. Put tiny goodies inside each piece.

2. Lay the wrapping paper facedown on a table. Set the three pieces in a row along the edge of the paper, with the long piece in the center. Leave a small space between each piece.

3. Tape the edge of the paper in a line across the tubes. Roll the paper over the tubes until they're covered. Trim off the extra paper and tape it in place. Tuck in the extra paper at each end to keep the treats inside.

4. Gently twist the tubes where you left the spaces. Using the straight pin, poke tiny holes around where you twisted, on both sides. This will make it easier to bust the popper open. Tie a piece of ribbon around the two twisted areas.

5. Bring the poppers to your party, and enjoy!

Other Ideas

- ❀ Insert a special picture or piece of paper that says "winner" inside one of the poppers. Whoever gets the note in his or her popper wins a prize.

- ❀ Make "fortune poppers" by inserting fortunes into the poppers from leftover fortune cookies—or make up fortunes of your own and write them on little pieces of paper.

- Likes to play air guitar while singing into her hairbrush.

- Wishes she could change her hair color as often as she changes her favorite band.

- Throws last-minute lip sync concerts at family holiday parties.

The **ROWDY ROCK STAR** rules. Ever since she graduated from baby food, she's known she was born for music. The rhymes and rhythms flow through her soul like oxygen in her body. You rock stars out there may be singing into your curling irons now, but you're getting ready to rock the planet. Before you make it big, stock up on the right gear, like the radical body riffs shown here.

Rock On! Guitar Strap

Mini Music Pins

SUPER FAN!

THE GREATEST ROCK STAR EVER!

LA ROSA

Guitar-Pick Charm Bracelet

Rock On! GUITAR STRAP

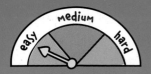

To be a rocker, you absolutely have to learn to play the guitar— first acoustic, then electric. And before you do that, you have to have the purrr-fect strap to match your gritty grooves. Let your inner kitty out with this fake-fur-trimmed treat. You'll be the envy of the stage. Important tip: Make sure your guitar has knobs for attaching a strap.

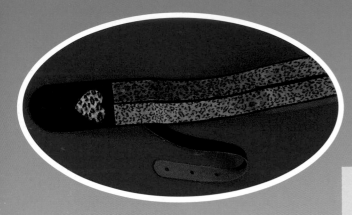

Stuff You'll Need

- standard guitar strap
- 1 yard of fake fur trim
- 2 fake fur heart patches
- E6000 glue
- scissors

How to Do It

1. Cut the fake-fur trim into two strips, each 17 inches long.

2. Rub some E6000 glue onto the backs of the two hearts. Place each heart facing "out" at both ends of the strap, just above the knob notch.

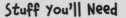

Other Ideas

- Instead of using two strips of fur, use one thick strip.

- Forget the fur and glue on letters or rhinestones that spell out "rock goddess" or "stage diva" or "princess."

- Use paint pens to stencil or draw your own designs.

- Sad because you want to be a rock star, but have no guitar? In the meantime, decorate a belt the same way as you would this strap. It will look just as cool.

3. Apply a bead of glue to the back of one of the fur strips and rub it from end to end. This strip will go in between the hearts, along the left side of the strap. Repeat the process for the other strip and place it on the right side, so the two strips are side by side. Rub your fingers over the strips to smooth out any bumps. Set them under a couple heavy books overnight for extra staying power.

Mini Music PINS

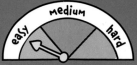

Mini pins are as hot as the concrete in an Arizona summer. They turn a nerdy shirt into a hipster one, not to mention the punch they give to backpacks, purses, guitar straps, bulletin boards, and jean jackets. The best pins are those that sport far-out pictures of bands and quirky sayings. Instead of searching the globe for these gems, make a collection of your own! Get your friends involved and swap 'em.

Stuff You'll Need

- wooden discs, each 1 inch in diameter (1 disc for each pin)
- music magazines
- craft acrylic paints in assorted colors and paintbrush
- ¾-inch pin backs (1 for each pin)
- Aleene's Original Tacky Glue
- E6000 glue
- scissors
- water-based varnish and brush

How to Do It

1. Paint one side of each wooden disc in a different color. Let dry.

2. Put short sayings together by cutting out words and photos from headlines in the magazines. Go for small type so it will fit on your pin.

3. Use the tacky glue to paste the words and images onto the painted discs. When you're done, brush a thin layer of tacky glue over the entire disc. This will act as sealer for the paper. Let dry.

4. Cover each disc with a layer of varnish and let dry.

5. Turn the discs over, facedown. Add a small glob of E6000 glue to the back of each disc and press a pin back in place. Let dry for several hours.

Other Ideas

- Don't make these pins only for music—you can also theme them to sports teams, movie stars, school groups, or anything else.
- Paste one letter on each disc, then line them up in a row to spell out a word.
- Instead of a pin back, glue on a magnet back and use on the fridge.

Guitar-Pick Charm BRACELET

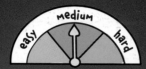
easy medium hard

Throughout the history of rock-'n'roll shows, one of the all-time prized possessions is the guitar pick thrown out to the crowd. Everyone cheers for the lucky fan who catches it in midair! Until that happens to you, go to your corner record or music store and pick up a handful of picks to make this totally far-out bracelet. Who knows, some day you may be the one throwing it out to the crowd!

Stuff You'll Need

- chain bracelet (found at the craft store)
- 10 guitar picks in different shapes and colors
- 10 small rhinestones in different shapes and colors
- 20 jump rings
- needle-nose pliers (optional)
- E6000 glue
- piece of card stock
- toothpick

How to Do It

1. Lay the picks in a row on the card stock. Pick them up one at a time and put a small glob of E6000 glue at the top. Place a jump ring so half of it is in the glue, and the other half is sticking out over the top of the pick. Do this for all the picks. Let dry for several hours.

2. Flip the picks over. Use the toothpick to dab a dot of glue on the back of one of the rhinestones. Set the rhinestone in the center of one of the picks. Repeat for the other picks. Let dry for about 30 minutes.

3. Lay out your picks in the order you want them to hang on the bracelet.

4. With your fingers, bend open the remaining 10 jump rings and hook them through the rings on the picks.

Tip

If you're handy with needle-nose pliers, they make it easier to open and close the jump rings. Otherwise, your fingers will work just fine.

5. One by one, attach each open jump ring to a link on the bracelet, then bend the jump ring shut. Keep going until you've attached all of the picks.

Words of Wisdom

Don't be scared to try something crazy. I once made a skirt out of neckties, and I really wanted to wear it to school. I was kind of new there, and I didn't want people to think I was nuts. I finally did wear it, and it was one of my best days ever. Every single person loved it!

—Rachel Pfeffer, 17, duct tape artist (www.luckyduct.com)

Other Ideas

- Glue a pin back to a decorated pick and wear it on your shirt or jacket.

- Glue a row of picks along the top of a smooth hair barrette.

- Instead of using picks for the bracelet, make some mini music pins (page 103). Glue jump rings onto their backs and attach those instead.

* Has a blister on her ear from yakking on the phone so much.

* Dreams of writing a gossip column for her school newspaper.

* Has more pen pals than her dad has ties.

Take-Along Scrapbook

Glitter Pens

Think of how ho-hum life would be without a social calendar to follow. No parties, no activities, no place to wear that killer outfit you bought at the mall. The sophisticated **SOCIAL BUTTERFLY** knows how crucial it is to keep everyone together and entertained. Cell phones, Palm Pilot, instant messaging, email, even snail mail—all are fair game when it comes to organization, friendship, and fun. Here are some projects to make the job easier.

Painted Cell-Phone Cover

Take-Along SCRAPBOOK

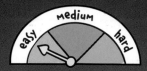

With your busy schedule, all those friends and everlasting memories can slip by in an instant. Capture the moments with a mini photo scrapbook. You can buy these little blank books at book and craft stores for less than five dollars each. Keep one in your backpack, locker, or purse to hold photos and for writing down notes, thoughts, and reminders.

Stuff You'll Need

* mini blank book, the size of a business card (or a small address book)
* small pictures or photos (preferably with sticky backs)
* assorted letter stickers or markers
* assorted pieces of patterned scrapbook paper (you can also use construction, wrapping, or magazine paper)
* sticker photo captions or pen
* glue stick
* scissors

How to Do It

1. Use the glue stick to seal together every other page. This will make your pages thick and sturdy.

2. Cut rectangles from the scrapbook paper that fit the size of the book pages. Glue one rectangle to each page. (You don't have to cover *all* of the pages. Leave some blank so you will have room to write.) Rub your finger over the paper to remove any lumps or glue bubbles.

3. Rub the glue stick onto the back of a picture (unless they already have sticky backs) and place it on a page.

4. Add a funny sticker caption or make one up and write it in with a pen.

5. Put letter stickers on the cover to name your mini scrapbook.

Other Ideas

* Make a photo phone book by putting pictures of your friends in the book with their phone numbers beneath each photo.

* Use the book for a private poem journal or secret diary. It's so small no one will find it!

Glitter PENS

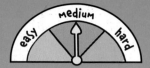

There's no better way to show someone you care than to sit down and write him or her a letter or card, old-school style. No, not via your personal computer or rubber-stamp collection. We're talking the pen-in-hand kind. Since you're going to such great lengths to prove your friendship, do it in style with one of these glamourous plastic pens.

Stuff You'll Need

* plastic ballpoint pens
* loose glitter in assorted colors
* paper plate
* double-sided tape
* paper
* scissors
* spray varnish and paper mask

How to Do It

1. Pour a small pile of glitter onto the paper plate.

2. Carefully stick a strip of the double-sided tape onto the pen, starting at one end and smoothing it down to the tip. Add more rows of tape until the entire pen is covered.

3. Hold the pen with one finger on each end and lay it in the plate of glitter. Roll it until the pen is totally covered. If you see any empty spots, pick up some glitter with your fingers and press it on. Tap the tip of the pen onto a piece of paper to get rid of any loose glitter flecks. Now blow on it to remove even more glitter flecks.

4. Pour the excess glitter from the plate onto a piece of paper. Now carefully pour it back into your glitter container. Fill your plate with a new color for your next pen and repeat steps 2–4.

5. Once you've covered as many pens as you want, take them outside and carefully spray them with a layer of varnish. Don't forget to wear your paper mask! Let dry for one hour before writing away.

Other Ideas

* It's super easy to make a pen with striped colors. Pick up a roll of double-sided tape that has a protective backing on one side. Leave the backing on as you lay the tape in strips down the pen, as in step 2. Now, remove the backing from *every other* strip and roll it in the glitter. Next, remove the backing from the remaining strips and roll your pen in a different color glitter. There you have it—striped writing utensils!

Hey! When using spray varnish, *always* put on a paper mask. Shake the can and then turn the nozzle in the direction that you are going to spray. Hold your item about two feet away from you and spray.

Painted CELL-PHONE Cover

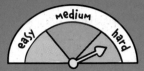

Your cell phone is practically an extension of your body, so shouldn't its design be as individual as you are? Besides, that Hello Kitty cover is starting to look pretty darn worn out. It's time to update and revamp. Plus, it will make the chatting, listening, crying, and laughing mean so much more!

Stuff You'll Need

* cell phone with removable cover
* craft acrylic paints in assorted colors and paintbrush
* blue low-tack masking tape (found in hardware stores)
* liner brush
* fine-grade sandpaper
* small safety pin
* water-based varnish and brush

Hey! Before you start this project, make sure you have a phone with a removable cover. If not, it's best to skip this one!

How to Do It

1. Remove the cover from the phone. Cover the clear window on *both* sides with the blue masking tape.

2. Lightly sand the front and sides of the cover so the paint will grip. Wipe off any dust.

3. Dip the brush in the paint and cover the entire cover with a color of your choice. Apply two more coats, letting each coat dry in between.

Tip

If you're too busy being the social gal you are to deal with steps 1–3, just pick up a new cell-phone cover in a color you like. Then jump right to step 4 and get decorating!

4. Add the details. Dip the safety pin in the paint and use it to make dots. Use the liner brush to make squiggles. Let dry.

5. Brush on a layer of varnish to seal the paint. Let it dry and then remove the blue tape from the window. If the blue tape leaves a smudge, use window cleaner and a tissue to clean it off. If the ear holes are covered with paint or varnish, use a safety pin to poke them clean. Now reattach your crazy new cover to your phone and dial up!

Words of Wisdom

Learn to enjoy the creative process. Your first, second, or third designs for something may look like crud to you, but you'll learn neat things from them. Step away from them and go do something else, and you will find your fourth try is more wonderful than you could have ever imagined.

—Michelle Bahr, 36, designer and artist (www.hipoli.com)

Other Ideas

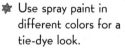

* Use spray paint in different colors for a tie-dye look.

* Use white glue to paste on little words or pictures from magazines. When dry, cover with a coat of varnish.

* If you have a cell phone that *doesn't* have a removeable cover, just carefully paint small designs around the holes and number keys.

Tip

After lots of chatting time, your paint may begin to rub off. No worries, just repaint it and add a new coat of varnish.

Spa Guru

- ◉ Gives and receives mini facials during lunchtime recess.

- ◉ Knows more about aromatherapy than algebra.

- ◉ Loves nothing better than a long, relaxing soak in the tub.

After a hard session of homework, a girl sure could use some relief. No one understands that better than SPA GURU, the queen of relaxation. So what's a crafty diva to do when her inner spa guru comes calling? No problemo! Get ready to be pampered like a princess once you whip together these super-sonic spa treatments. They're just like the stuff in expensive boutiques, only better because you'll have made them from scratch to match your independent style.

Tingly Tootsies Foot Scrub

Wacky Wire Scrubber Set

Scent-Sational Sachets

Tingly Tootsies FOOT SCRUB

Whether you're a couch potato or an after-school athlete, those tootsies need some serious TLC. Before you polish your toes and slip on some sandals, take a few minutes to indulge. All you need are three simple ingredients to deliver two sweet-smelling, yummy-feeling, good-lookin' feet.

Stuff You'll Need

- ½ cup olive oil
- ½ cup fine sea salt (found at the grocery store)
- 3 drops peppermint essential oil
- mixing bowl
- spoon
- towel
- empty glass or plastic jar with lid (optional)
- letter stickers (optional)

How to Do It

1. Combine the olive oil, sea salt, and peppermint oil in the bowl and mix thoroughly with the spoon. Set aside.

2. Fill your bathtub or sink with enough warm water to cover your feet. Soak those twinkle toes for three to five minutes. Close your eyes and let the stress of the day drift away while your heels soften.

3. Remove your feet and pat them dry with the towel. Lay the towel flat on the floor or on a step stool. Put your feet over the towel and rub the soothing mixture all over each foot in a circular motion to scrub that dry skin right away!

4. Place your feet back in the tub or sink, wash 'em off, and dry 'em with the towel. For the grand finale, place those freshly scrubbed tootsies into your favorite (and comfortable, of course!) sling-back shoes.

Other Ideas

- Put the scrub in a pretty jar to give as a gift (or to keep for yourself!). Clean the jar in warm, soapy water first, then let dry. Mix up the scrub and put it in the jar. Seal tightly, then decorate the jar with the letter stickers.

Wacky Wire SCRUBBER SET

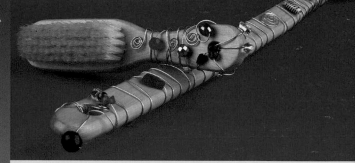

One good way to refresh yourself is to scrub away dead skin and dirt. Sounds gross, but it's a relaxing treat when you use a lovely bejeweled scrubber set. Wirework like this sells in fancy boutiques for big bucks, but with a little patience you can wrap circles around the idea for next to nothing.

Stuff You'll Need

- back scrubber and/or foot scrubber
- roll of 20-gauge wire
- assorted glass or plastic beads
- needle-nose pliers

How to Do It

1. Use the cutting tool on your needle-nose pliers to cut several pieces of wire, each 5 inches long. For the foot scrubber, plan on using two or three pieces of wire. For the back scrubber, you'll need nine or ten pieces.

2. Take one piece of wire and put the needle-nose pliers at one end. Use the pliers to bend the wire into a circle. Keep twisting it three times until you have a tight-looking spiral.

3. Place the spiral flat against the handle of the foot or back scrubber, just under the brush. Hold it in place with your thumb and use your other hand to wrap the wire tightly around the handle one time.

4. Slide a bead onto the wire, then wrap the wire around again. The bead should sit on top of the handle. Add another bead, then wrap the wire around again.

Tip

Use one hand to hold the wire in place on the handle while the other hand wraps the new wire around. This takes practice—don't worry if it doesn't feel comfortable at first. As you wrap, move the beads around until you like the way they look.

5. Continue wrapping and adding beads until you have only 1 inch left of the wire. Make another spiral to finish it off, like you did in step 1.

6. Repeat steps 2–5 until you reach the end of the handle.

Other Ideas

- Use different colors of wire and add more than one bead at a time.
- Ditch the wire altogether and use extra-strength craft glue to attach bright gems or rhinestones.

Scent-sational SACHETS

One of the fun things about being a girl is collecting all kinds of delicious-smelling accessories. There's no better place to start than with sweet-smelling sachets (sa-SHAYS) for your dresser drawer or bedroom closet, where they'll waft their delicate perfume all over your clothes. Before you start on this project, get familiar with the many scents there are to choose from. For example, lavender is ahhhh, so soothing for your mind, while tangy, fruity smells may make you hungry. Only you know what you like, so take some time to stop and smell the sachet packages at the store!

Stuff You'll Need

- sachet filling (dried lavender, pine needles, potpourri, or a sachet packet bought at a craft store)
- fabric
- piece of ribbon, 20 inches long
- twine or heavy thread
- small flowers or decorative charms
- Aleene's OK To Wash-It fabric glue
- scissors

How to Do It

1. Cut the fabric into a rectangle that is 5 inches × 10 inches.

Tip When choosing a fabric, pick one that's soft and foldable, but still heavy enough to hold glue. Cotton and silk are two good options.

2. Lay the fabric facedown on the table, with one of the short sides nearest you. Squeeze a line of glue (not too much, steady dabs are best) along the top and fold over about ¼ inch of fabric to make a seam. Hold it in place until the fabric sticks. Do the same thing along the bottom.

3. Flip your fabric over so that the seams face down. Squeeze a line of glue from the top to about halfway down on both sides. Fold the fabric in half, pressing down on the glued parts until the fabric holds. You should now have a pocket that is glued together at the sides, with seams at the top. Let this dry for about 1 hour.

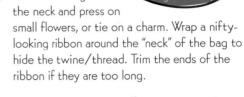

4. Very carefully turn the pocket inside out. This is your sachet bag (all seams should now be inside)! Fill it with whatever you like: pine needles, dried lavender, potpourri, or a sachet packet. Be careful not to put too much inside or it may separate your glued seams. Tie the top closed with twine or heavy thread, making it tight so that there will be no leaks.

5. Add a dab of glue to the neck and press on small flowers, or tie on a charm. Wrap a nifty-looking ribbon around the "neck" of the bag to hide the twine/thread. Trim the ends of the ribbon if they are too long.

> **Tip**
>
> After a couple weeks, the sachet's fragrance will fade. When that happens, simply open the bag, empty it, and refill with fresh sachet.

Other Ideas

- Embellish the front of your sachet by adding a pretty patch.
- Aside from using it to freshen up your closet and dresser drawers, place the sachet in your school locker, bathroom cabinet, or suitcase when you travel.

Lazy-Girl Sachet

If you'd rather take the quick and easy route, pick up a sachet bag that's already sealed and ready to go (ribbon and all!)—they're easy to find at most craft stores. Before adding the sachet mix, squeeze a small line of glue along the bottom of the bag and press on a layer of beaded trim. If you want, glue some trim around the top, too. Let dry for 1 hour. Pour in your favorite sachet mix and simply pull the strings tight. Hang it in your closet or on your bedroom door handle.

- ✿ OWNS more jerseys and jogging suits than dresses and skirts.

- ✿ Has dreamed of owning a sports bra since she was five.

- ✿ Plasters her room, notebook, and locker with pictures of her favorite sports idols.

Leave it to the SPORTY SISTA to come to the rescue. She's always the one to score that last point, not only winning the game but sending the team to the championships. This soon-to-be superstar is destined for greatness—the only problem is choosing a sport to focus on, because right now she loves them all! If you're the type who can't wait to hit the field, here are three sporty accessories to help you win the game in style.

Verbal Visor

High-Impact Sneakers

Duct-Tape Coin Purse

Verbal VISOR

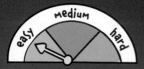

Sometimes less is more. Especially when it comes to wearing stuff with words on your head. Take this visor, for example. We like it how it is, clean and sleek. All it needs is a bit of personality. Choose a simple word or phrase to liven it up. I'll betcha no one else will have one like it.

Stuff You'll Need

- fabric visor
- letters (you can use rub-on transfers, stencils and paint, glue-on letters, or fabric pens)
- Aleene's Original Tacky Glue (if needed)
- pencil (if needed)

How to Do It

1. Lay your visor flat on a table so the front is facing you. Place your letters or stencil on the front panel and center them so you will know exactly where to apply them. If you're drawing freehand, practice on paper and then lightly sketch your letters onto the visor with a pencil.

2. Add your first letter. If using a stencil, tape the stencil to the front panel, then dab your brush in the paint and "pounce" it in an up-and-down motion over the stencil. If using glue-on letters, apply glue to the back surface of each letter and press in place on the hat. If using rub-on transfers, follow the directions on the package. Let dry for a few seconds. Work your way from left to right, adding letters until you are done.

3. If you want, add other accents around the word or on the visor area. Draw swirls or flowers with fabric pens, or use fabric glue to add rhinestones.

Other Ideas

- Instead of letters, glue on a piece of cool trim—maybe one that matches your team uniform.
- Pick up a plastic visor instead and use paint pens to decorate the see-through brim.

High-Impact SNEAKERS

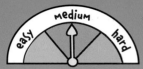

Why paint your shoes? Well, why not paint your shoes? Hold on! Before you go putting polka dots all over your beautiful new boots, you should know we're talking sneakers. It's almost as if the plain white canvas kind was created just to be decorated. Ask permission to paint your shoes first, then pick your favorite color and get busy.

Stuff You'll Need

- pair of white canvas sneakers
- craft acrylic paint in various colors (shown here are three shades of pink, accented with white)
- small foam brush
- white micro glitter (optional)
- small rubber stamps (optional)
- pencil and paper
- liner brush
- water-based varnish and brush

How to Do It

1. Sketch out your design on paper. Think about where you want to place the colors. Paint looks different wet than dry, so put a dab of each color on your paper and let it dry to see what it will look like. You can paint different sections of your shoes different shades, or do the entire shoe one color.

2. Paint the tongues on both shoes and let them dry. Now move on to the outside of the shoe, working section by section. When you're done, let the whole thing dry.

3. Don't forget the rubber base! You can paint this area, too, though, sadly, it will scrape off someday, even if you put a hundred coats of varnish on it. But that's okay, you can just refresh your work every so often. Let dry.

4. Use an accent color (white works great) to paint on stars, stripes, or hearts. Before the paint is dry, sprinkle a little micro glitter over it for a touch of sparkle. Let dry.

5. Cover all the painted areas of the shoes with a layer of the water-based varnish. Let dry. Then find a pair of new laces and tie those puppies up!

Other Ideas

- To be really crazy, use white craft glue to decoupage comic-book pictures on your canvas shoes.

- Paint a tote bag to match.

Duct-Tape COIN PURSE

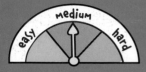

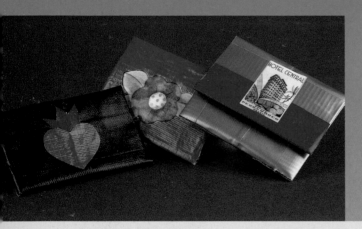

Duct tape isn't just for fixing pipes anymore. The silver stuff and all its brightly colored companions have entered mainstream fashion by way of handmade purses, wristbands, even prom dresses. Curious? Learn what all the hype is about by starting with this simple coin purse. It's ultra nifty because it's small enough to slide in your sock, shoe, or pocket, but big enough to hold lunch money, a key, and lip balm.

Stuff You'll Need

- roll of duct tape (can be found at the dollar, hardware, or discount department store)
- strip of Velcro with adhesive backing, 1 inch long
- stickers (vinyl or plastic are best) and/or duct tape in other colors (optional)
- brand-new pair of scissors
- measuring tape or ruler

How to Do It

1. Begin by making a double-sided strip of duct tape. Cut two strips of duct tape, each 9 inches long. Lay one strip down, sticky side up. Lay the second strip next to it, also sticky side up, with a bit of its long edge overlapping the long edge of the first strip.

2. Cut two more strips in the same color, also 9 inches long. Lay one strip, sticky side down, on top of the first strip from step 1. Lay the other strip, also sticky side down, on top of the second strip from step 1. If you have some overlap on the ends, trim it with the scissors.

3. Lay your double-sided strip on the table so the short side is nearest you. Fold the bottom end up 3 inches.

4. Cut off another piece of duct tape, 3 inches long. With the sticky side facing up, cut that strip in half lengthwise. Now you have two skinny strips. Use one to close each side of the folded-over part of the big strip. Your coin purse is now intact! Fold over the top flap and trim the edge so it looks nice and even.

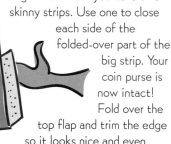

Tip

Duct tape is way sticky. It's easier to cut straight lines if you keep the sticky side up. If your coin purse comes out a bit wrinkly, just add another layer of tape on top to cover the bumps.

5. Take the Velcro and peel off the protective backing on both sides. Place it at the edge of the flap on the inside. Then close the flap and press the Velcro in place. The Velcro will keep your things from falling out.

Tip

Paper stickers will easily rub off. If you want your purse to look good even after being stuffed in your sweaty gym socks, use vinyl or plastic stickers.

6. Decorate the purse with vinyl stickers or with shapes cut out from other colors of duct tape.

Other Ideas

🌸 Make a long skinny strap for your coin purse and you can wear it across your chest. Just cut a piece of duct tape 24 inches long, then roll it tightly lengthwise until it looks like a spaghetti strap. To attach the strap to the purse, cut two more pieces of tape, each 3 inches long, and use them to stick the strap to the inner sides of the purse.

🌸 To make a larger purse, just double all of the measurements.

🌸 Put an extra pocket on your purse. Just make a small double-sided layer of duct tape (as you did in steps 1 and 2), then tape the sides and bottom to the outside of the purse.

Surf Girl

- Can pack a beach tote with her eyes closed in sixty seconds flat.

- Prefers brand name surfboards to brand name handbags.

- Actually knows what it means to "hang 10."

Crashing waves, funky swimsuits, sand crunching between your toes—this is the gnarly life of the **SURF GIRL**. Even if she's never actually *tried* surfing, she knows it's only a matter of time. Until then, it's all about appreciating the beach, the rays, and the laid-back style. Sadly, every day can't revolve around surfboards, sun, and waves. So here are some righteous rainy-day projects to keep those sandy fingers busy 'til the sun returns.

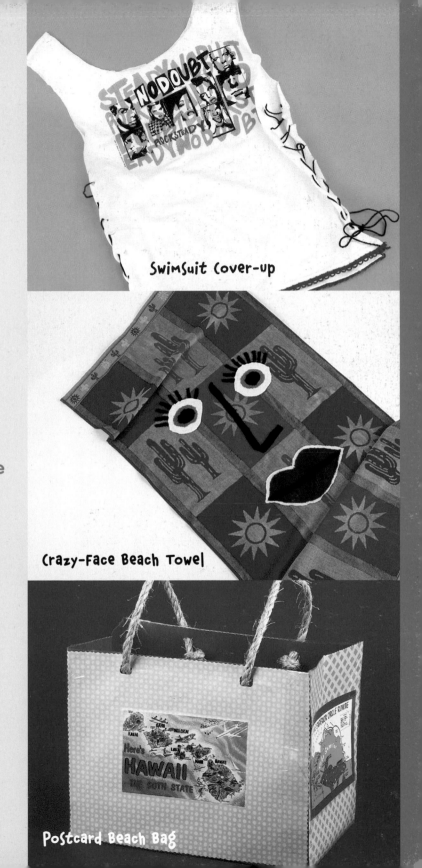

Swimsuit Cover-up

Crazy-Face Beach Towel

Postcard Beach Bag

Swimsuit COVER-UP

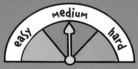

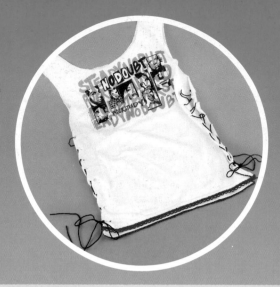

It's one of the universe's unanswered questions: Why are concert T-shirts made so dang huge? Even the smallest size hangs down to our knees. Don't dwell on it. Instead, pull out your scissors and a set of shoelaces, and transform it into a rockin' swimsuit cover-up. While everyone else is wearing boring terrycloth robes, you'll be the grooviest gal on the beach.

Stuff You'll Need

- large T-shirt
- pair of shoelaces, 70 inches long
- pencil
- straight pins
- scissors

How to Do It

1. You'll need to cut off the sleeves and collar of the shirt to make it into a tank top. To do this, take the pencil and lightly sketch a half-circle around and below the collar. Do the same around the arm seams. Once it looks right, cut off the collar and sleeves.

2. Pin the open sides of the shirt together, 2 inches in from the seam. Remove the side seam by cutting next to the pins, up the side of the shirt all the way to the armhole. (Be sure to cut through both layers.) Throw away the seam. Repeat on the other side of the shirt. Remove the pins.

3. Starting with one side, hold both layers and make a vertical fold up the side of the shirt. Use the scissors to snip small nips through both layers, all the way down the fold. Space the holes about 3 inches apart. When you're done, undo the fold and lay the shirt flat.

4. Thread one of the shoelaces through the top two holes so it goes through the front and back layer. Loosely lace it like you would a pair of shoes, all the way down. When you get to the bottom, tie it off with a double-knotted bow. It's okay if the laces are long and hang down a bit—it looks good that way! Repeat steps 3 and 4 for the other side of the shirt.

Tip If you want the cover-up to fit tighter, cut more off the sides when you cut off the seam. If you want it shorter, cut material from the bottom.

Other Ideas

- You can also use colored shoelaces, which can be found at the craft store.

Crazy-Face BEACH TOWEL

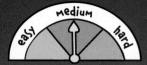

No swimming ensemble is complete without the ever-popular beach towel. As the years pass, towels that have seen better days always start piling up and taking up space. Here's a way to put them to good use: Simply cut them up in the name of art!

Stuff You'll Need

- big beach towel
- assorted old towels in different colors (ask permission first!)
- Aleene's Fray No More
- Aleene's OK To Wash-It fabric glue
- 6 sheets of paper and pencil
- scissors

How to Do It

1. Sketch out a simple face on a sheet of paper: two circles for the eyes, two for the pupils, a triangle for the nose, and an oval for the mouth. If you want a really crazy face, make the eyes uneven, the nose really long, or the mouth curvy.

2. Take another sheet of paper and, using your sketch as a guide, draw the eye as big as you want it on the towel. Draw each feature on a separate sheet of paper. Cut out the shapes.

3. Pin each shape onto an old towel and cut them out. Repeat until all of the features are cut out.

4. Lay your big towel out flat. Arrange the features on the towel until you like the way they look. Pick up one eye and squeeze the fabric glue all over the back of it (especially along the edges), then set it back in place. Rub it with your hands to squish the glue in place and smooth out any ripples. Continue gluing on the rest of the pieces.

5. Take the bottle of Aleene's Fray No More and run a line of it around the edge of each face feature. This will keep the cut edges from fraying in the washer and dryer. You can wash the towel as usual in the washing machine.

Other Ideas

- If you feel confident, try making the eyes so one is winking. To do this, cut one eye in the shape of an oval (instead of a circle). Add small rectangles pointing down for the eyelashes.

Postcard BEACH BAG

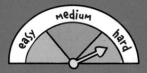

Sunscreen, check. Beach towel, check. Sunglasses, check. Once you've gathered the essentials, you'll need something super-trendy to carry them in. Look no further than this postcard beach bag. It's made out of colored card stock, old vacation postcards (bought at a yard sale), and clear contact paper. It looks awesome when it's finished, but it's a bit of a chore to assemble. If you need an extra set of hands, ask your brother, sister, cousin, or family pet (well, maybe not the pet) for some help. Remind them of the favor they owe you from way back when....

Stuff You'll Need

- 3 pieces of colored or patterned card stock, each $8\frac{1}{2}$ x 11 inches
- 4 vacation postcards, old or new
- roll of clear contact paper (found at the grocery store)
- clear packing tape

- 2 pieces of jute or thick nylon cording, each 12 inches long
- hole puncher
- ruler
- pencil
- glue stick
- scissors

How to Do It

1. Lay a piece of card stock horizontally on the table. Measure it into thirds (each should be about $3\frac{1}{2}$ x $8\frac{1}{2}$ inches). Mark the lines with a pencil. Cut along the lines, so you have three pieces. Set one piece aside.

2. Take the two "cut" pieces and lay them vertically on the table. Cover the back of one postcard with the glue stick and center it on one of the pieces of card stock. Press it in place and rub your fingers over it to remove any bubbles. Do the same for the other piece of card stock.

3. Now get the two larger sheets of card stock, the ones you didn't cut. Lay them on the table horizontally. Glue a postcard in the center of each one. You now have the four sides of your bag. The two larger panels are the front and back; the two smaller panels are the sides.

4. Unroll the contact paper and cut a piece 12 inches long. Lay it flat on the table, shiny side down. Carefully peel away the protective backing. Place the front panel of the bag (postcard side down) on the sticky surface of the contact paper, near the bottom edge. Fold the protective backing back down over the panel and rub it with your fingers to smooth out any bubbles. Cut away excess contact paper. Repeat the process for the other three panels.

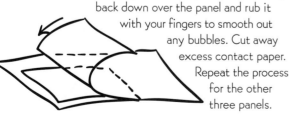

5. Go and get that extra piece of card stock you set aside in step 1. That's the bottom of your bag. Cover that with contact paper, too. Now all the panels are covered, front and back, with clear contact paper. Right on! We're finally ready to put it all together.

6. Take the front panel and one of the side panels and line them up vertically, postcard sides out. (Make sure the tops of the postcards are all facing up.) Cut off a 9-inch strip of packing tape. Carefully connect the two panels by placing half of the tape on each edge, so they are joined. Keep doing this until all four panels are connected.

7. Use more strips of the packing tape to attach the bottom. Add strips of tape to the inside of the bag as well, wherever edges come together, to make your bag super strong.

8. Add a line of the packing tape all around the top of the bag, so it will be extra durable. Take the hole puncher and punch two holes in the front, about 2 inches down from the top. Do the same on the back. If you need to make larger holes for the jute to fit through, make more punches.

> **Tip**
>
> If you plan on carrying heavy items in your bag, make the holes sturdier by using a grommet tool. It will add thick silver rings to the holes to prevent them from tearing.

9. String a piece of jute through the two holes on one side and tie each end in a knot, as shown. Repeat for the other side.

Other Ideas

🐚 This bag is styled for the beach, but you can also make bags themed for fashion, cooking, sports, school, or whatever you like to do.

* Has three celebrity autograph books and two of them are filled.

* Gets all her important daily news from "Entertainment Tonight" and "Access Hollywood."

* Covers her locker with pictures of her fave movie heartthrobs.

Every female is a starry-eyed teenager at heart. We love soaking up the latest gossip about our favorite movie, TV, and music stars. But the TEENYBOPPER goes one step further—she visits or sets up online fan sites, is bold enough to ask for autographs, and plasters her walls with layers of posters and souvenirs. For hardcore teen queens like you, there's no such thing as too much memorabilia—so here's even more!

Kitschy Clock

Matchbox Pop Star Shrines

Embroidered Dream Pillow

Kitschy CLOCK

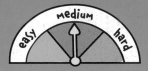

Credit: Sugar Magazine/Hachette Filipacchi UK Ltd.

Magazine covers are more than just flashy pictures and sizzling headlines. They are also a bold art form designed to catch our attention. And boy, do they ever. Some covers have so much flair that they could be framed and hung on the wall. You're going to one-up that and make the cover of your favorite mag into a useful, kitschy-looking clock.

Stuff You'll Need

* thin piece of foam board, 13 x 10 inches
* magazine cover
* battery-operated clock mechanism with short hands (found at the craft store)
* fake fur trim, 1½ yards long
* squeeze-on glitter
* string of beads or piece of yarn, 20 inches long
* glue stick
* Aleene's Original Tacky Glue or white craft glue
* E6000 glue
* ruler
* scissors

How to Do It

1. Cut the cover off of the magazine and rub the glue stick all over the back. Set it in the center of the foam board and press down. Smooth out any lumps or bubbles.

2. Add some squeeze glitter here and there on the cover to make it sparkle. Let dry.

3. Find the bottom left-hand corner of the cover. Measure 3 inches up, then 3 inches to the right. Make a dot in that spot. Poke your scissors through the dot and make a hole for the clock mechanism to fit through.

4. Open the clock package and follow the directions to put it together. Assemble the clock through the hole.

5. Squeeze a line of glue on the foam board, just outside the edge of the cover. Lay the fur trim on top of the glue. Cut off extra trim. Let dry.

6. Flip your new clock over, facedown. Put two globs of E6000 glue on the back, as shown. Lay the string of beads or yarn along the top, each end in a glob. Let dry. Hang and enjoy!

Other Ideas

* Instead of a magazine, use a cover from a book, record, or CD.

Tip If the hands of your clock are hard to see against the cover, carefully cover them with craft acrylic paint. It'll make a big difference!

Matchbox Pop-Star SHRINES

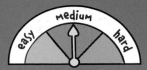

easy · medium · hard

Come on, admit it! You have a secret crush on some dreamy superstar that makes you break out in goose bumps every time you see his face. There's no harm in whipping up one of these mini matchbox shrines to place on top of your computer, locker shelf, or nightstand. But whatever you do, don't keep it under your pillow. That would just be too weird!

Hey! Before you empty the matchbox, ask an adult what you should do with the loose matches. If there are no adults around to ask, put the matches in a tin container (like a mint tin or coffee can) for safekeeping.

Stuff You'll Need

* small empty matchbox with sliding sleeve
* mini magazine photo of your superstar
* wooden rectangle, 2 x 1½ inches (found in craft stores)
* sequins
* craft acrylic paints in assorted colors and paintbrush
* loose or squeeze-on glitter
* Aleene's Original Tacky Glue
* scissors

How to Do It

1. Slide off the sleeve of the matchbox. Cut off the sleeve's two skinny sides and throw them away. You should be left with two pieces of cardboard. Paint one side of each and let dry.

2. Cut one of the painted pieces in half lengthwise to make two strips. Use the other painted piece to cut out a triangle. Set them aside.

3. Paint the matchbox inside and out. Paint the wooden rectangle, too. Let dry.

4. Glue the photo inside the matchbox and press to smooth out any bubbles.

5. Add a thin line of glue to the left, right, and top edges of the matchbox. Place a painted cardboard strip along each side edge. Press the triangle along the top edge. Hold each piece in place for a few minutes until it sets. Lay the matchbox on its back until dry.

6. Decorate the inside and outside of the matchbox with glitter, painted designs, and sequins.

7. Put a dab of glue on the bottom of the matchbox and set it in the middle of the wood rectangle. Hold for a few minutes. Let dry for 1 hour.

Embroidered Dream PILLOW

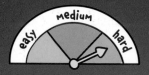

Those last few minutes in bed, just before you drift off to sleep each night, are great times to think about the highs and lows of the day, as well as the stuff you're looking forward to tomorrow. It's also a good time to close your eyes and imagine that Justin Timberlake is singing you a romantic love song. A girl can dream, right? Those deep sleep visions will feel even better when resting your pretty head on this fluffy pillow.

Stuff You'll Need

* ❋ pillowcase
* ❋ embroidery floss in assorted colors
* ❋ embroidery hoop and needle
* ❋ 2 buttons
* ❋ pencil and paper (or stencil)

How to Do It

1. Sketch out your design on a piece of paper, or trace the template on page 142. Letters are easy, so come up with a short phrase like "Sweet Dreams," "Dream on, dream away," or "Do not disturb."

2. Lightly draw your design or phrase on the border of the pillowcase. If you don't want to draw freehand, lay a stencil on the fabric and trace through the letters with a pencil.

3. Unscrew the embroidery hoop so you have two circles. Place the designed part of the pillowcase over the smaller

hoop. Place the larger hoop on top. Screw the two hoops together. This will keep the fabric nice and tight as you work. (Make sure only the designed layer is screwed into the hoop—you don't want to sew the pillowcase shut by accident!)

4. Cut one color of the floss into a piece 24 inches long. Thread it through the needle, pulling it through until one side is long and the other is a 2-inch tail. Tie a double knot at the end of the long side.

5. Use a "split stitch" to embroider the letters. See below to learn how. Keep going until you have only 1 inch of thread left, hanging out from underneath. Pull the needle off the thread, flip over the fabric, and separate the remaining thread into two pieces. Tie these two pieces in a double knot. Then thread your needle and start again, picking up where you left off.

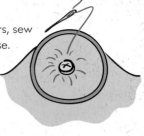

7. When you're done with your letters, sew a button on each side of the phrase. Then put the fabric back in the embroidery hoop and make easy line stitches around the button. Do one color at a time. These will look like little starbursts.

> **Tip**
>
> This project may take you a whole day, week, or even a month! Just work on it a little at a time. Find a small box to keep all your supplies in, so when you feel like stitching, it will be ready to go. You can work on it in the car during long road trips or while waiting at the doctor's office. And it's perfectly fine if your letters look uneven—that adds to the handmade charm.

> **Tip**
>
> Keep it simple. You don't have to cut your thread between letters. As you finish one letter, just jump over to the next on the underside of the fabric. Practice on a piece of scrap fabric first if you like. Don't worry if you make a mistake—just snip the thread, pull it out, and start over.

Other Ideas

* Embroider little stitches in the shape of stars on the body of the pillowcase.

* Embroider a design or phrase on the border of your sheet, too, for a matching bed set.

* Once you get the hang of it, try adding fun designs to blouses, pant legs, or backpacks, or make name napkins for the family table.

6. Continue until you've covered the whole design with stitches. If your design or phrase is bigger than what fits inside the hoop, do as much as you can, then open the screws and slide your fabric over. Tighten the screws back up and keep going.

How to Do the "Split Stitch"

1. Bring the needle up through the fabric.

2. Move the needle a bit further, in whatever direction you want the embroidered design to go, then poke the needle back down through the fabric.

3. Poke the needle back up, this time bringing it through the *middle* of the thread in the last stitch. You're "splitting" that stitch in two.

4. Move the needle a bit further along your design, then poke it back down again. Repeat steps 3 and 4.

DOODLING 101: A Crash Course

You're probably already into doodling—on your notebook, on your jeans, on the palms of your hands. But do you find yourself drawing the same old tired cubes and curlicues over and over? If so, stretch your sketching skills by trying these step-by-step doodles and letters.

flowers

Skull

leaf

fish

girl

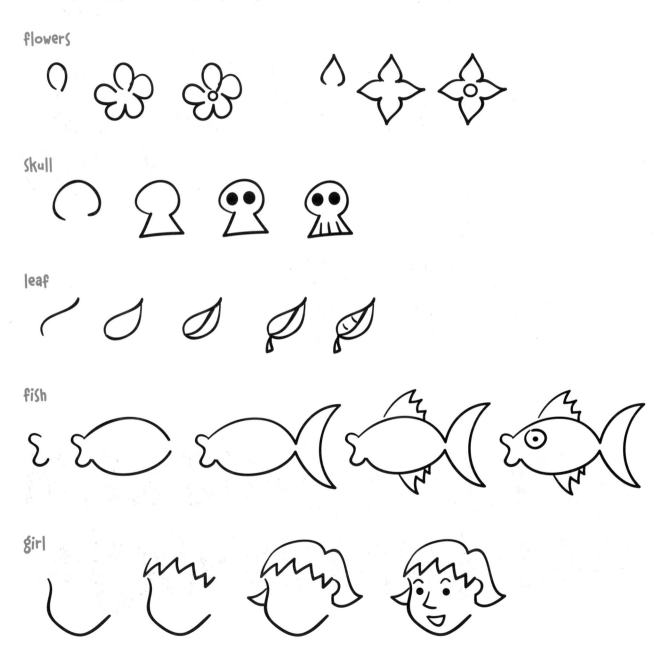

cherries

dog

grapes

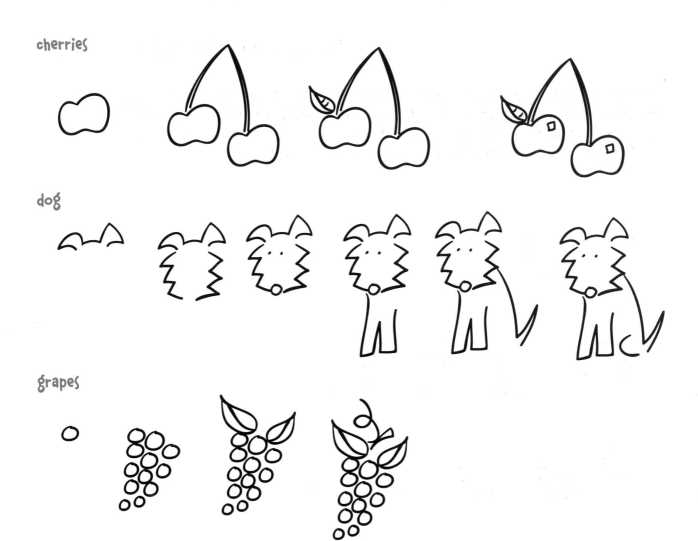

aBCDEFgHiJkLM
NOPQRStUVWXYZ

Clip Art Treasure Chest

Hungry for more pictures? Transfer, trace, or photocopy these dandy doodles to use on projects throughout the book.

Journal Page

Here's a blank page for you to make notes, practice doodles, or copy other art you find that you want to use in your projects.

Mystery Mask Template

Trace this template for the MYSTERY MASK project on page 44.

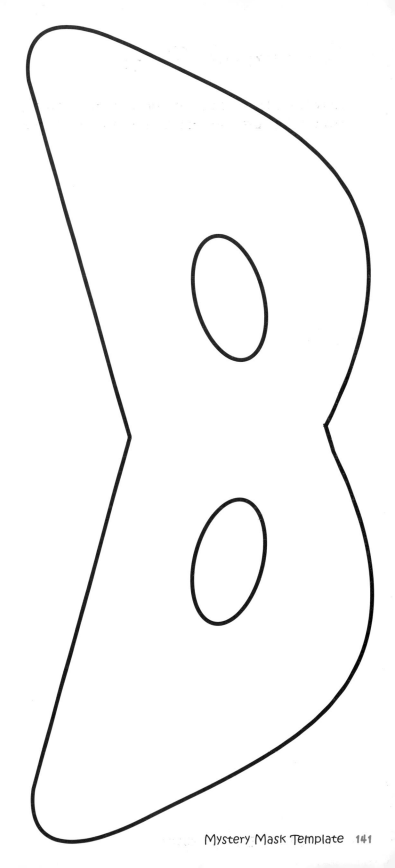

Sweet Dreams Template

Trace this template for the EMBROIDERED DREAM PILLOW project on page 134.

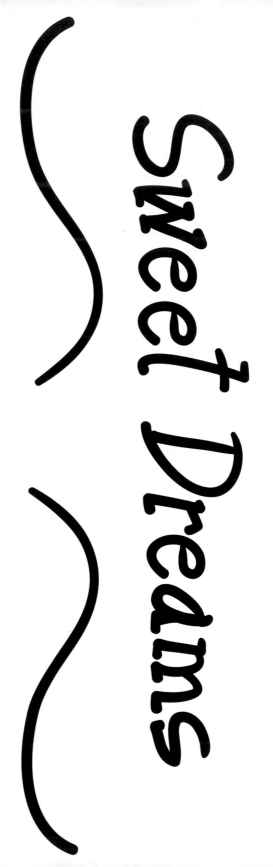

RESOURCES:
Where to Get Stuff

Wondering where to shop for all those unique supplies? Read on, sister. Below you will find a golden list of stores, outlets, and Web sites that are stocked with everything from cool-looking papers to glitter-enhanced paints.

Diane Ribbon and Notions

Mail-order craft supplies

Call (602) 271-9273 for a catalog.

Duncan Crafts

Makers of Aleene's glue line and Tulip Fabric Glitter Spray

For questions and tips on using their products, visit www.duncancrafts.com.

eBay

Assorted supplies to buy on the Web

To order, visit www.ebay.com.

Jo-Ann Fabric and Crafts

Fabric, trims, and general supplies

For the store nearest you, visit www.joann.com.

Michael's

General craft supplies.

For the store nearest you, visit www.michaels.com.

Stampington & Company

Unique collection of pictures, rubber stamps, bracelet blanks, and other goodies

To order, visit www.stampington.com.

Target

Go here to get clothing items, towels, a wire brush set, a light set, stackable CD shelves, and a bathroom accessories set.

For the store nearest you, visit www.target.com.

Wal-Mart

Visit this site for a table-and-glass-top set, as well as for general craft supplies.

Visit www.walmart.com to find the store nearest you.

Acknowledgments

Special thanks to my husband, Patrick, and our son, DeAngelo, for putting up with so many take-out dinners and excited-to-nervous-to-crazy mood swings on an hourly basis. A big high-five to my eleven-year-old daughter, Maya, who served as my personal "in-house consultant" on the ideas and text in this book. Lord knows she was the harshest critic ever! Glitter sprinkles to Julie Mazur, my editor, for inviting me to take on this project, and to Carrie Wheeler for her girl-friendly illustrations. A huge hug of gratitude to John Samora for being so nice about finding ways to photograph glitter, varnish, and glow-in-the-dark clay. *Muchos besos* to Pink Design for making it all come together so gloriously. A gold star to Emma and Abbey Ignaszewski, Madelyn McCaleb, and my crafty friends at GetCrafty.com for providing *mucho* inspiration. Thank you to my friends and family for listening to all my crazy adventures and ideas for the book: Theresa Cano; David and Michelle Cano; the crew at Diane Ribbon and Notions; the Murillo, Garcia, and Hadley families; Laurie Notaro; Randy Cordova; Anita Mabante Leach; Michelle Craig; Connie Midey; John Stanley; Michelle Savoy; Megan Bates; my mom-in-law, Suzie; and my mom and dad, Norma and David Cano.

I'd also like to thank the following artists for their contributions to various projects in this book: Tracy Dove (Flower "Empower" Pots and Botanical Bubble Wand); Holly Harrison (Scent-sational Sachets); Jane Malone (Scrabble Photo Magnets, Stamped Sticker Sheets, and Tin Time Capsules); Janice Taylor (Fortune Cookie Frame); Jennifer Enriquez (Roundabout Rings); Kerith Henderson (Bubblegum Soap Bars); Lara Piu (Tingly Tootsies Foot Scrub); and Maya Murillo (Glow-in-the-Dark Baubles).

Most of all, kudos to all the little crafty divas out there for having a glitter addiction as strong as mine—strong enough to warrant this book!